THE STRANGE TALE OF JESSE JONES AND THE WITCHES' TRIP TO EGYPT

JESSE JONES

FRONT COVER DESIGN-ALICE THOMPSON

Preface

Tis strange, - but true; for truth is always strange;
Stranger than fiction if it could be told,
How much would novels gain by the exchange!
How differently the world would men behold
(Byron)

The strange journey of Jesse Jones continues as she tries to publish her first book and CD in between hospital visits, playing the violin, complicated relationships, crazy housemates and everyday drama. Looking back life seemed quite normal, but that of course was before the Witch.

The Witch holds the key to something significant in Jesse's life, and only by continuing on her musical journey will Jesse find out what it is. There are old and new friends who lend a hand along the way and some, like George, who just add to the chaos. This is the second book in the series The Strange Tale of Jesse Jones, set in the beautiful countryside of Wales.

Contents

Chapter 1. Sore Eye 4-22

Chapter 2. Sore Brain 23-40

Chapter 3. Sore Fingers 41-63

Chapter 4. Old Haunts 64-88

Chapter 5. Parting of the Ways 89-99

Chapter 6. The Witch 100-121

Chapter 7. Bird 122-134

Chapter 8. New Directions 135-157

Chapter 9. George 158-179

Chapter 10. Vacation 180-201

Chapter 11. The Curse of the Tiger Cat 202-225

Chapter 12. Shades of Grey 226-243

Chapter 13. The Fifth Dimension 244-260

Postscript 261

Chapter1. Sore Eye

It is not foresight or hindsight we need. We need sight, plain and simple. We need to see what is right in front of us.
(Real Live Preacher)

"Where the fuck are we?" said Jules sounding exasperated. Jules used the f word a lot, not only as an expletive, but also as an adjective, and as general punctuation in her conversation; it seemed to carry more weight than a comma. "I'm not sure," I said hesitantly.

We seemed to have been travelling west for hours and there was no indication that we were any closer to our destination of Singleton Hospital in Swansea. We both became aware of Doris, the Sat Nav, babbling on in the back ground.

"Do you trust her?" said Jules frowning.

There was a pause as we both listened to Doris's confusing instructions.

"No!" We spoke together and Doris was unanimously fired. I detached her from her life support machine (the cigarette lighter) and we decided to try the more traditional method of navigation using signposts. When the next one appeared I realised my earlier mistake, which had contributed to our current predicament.

"It's the wrong town beginning with C."

I had been vaguely aware of seeing signs indicating a town beginning with the letters 'CAR' as we drove along and assumed it must be Carmarthen, on route to Swansea. Unfortunately I was so busy chatting to Jules I hadn't bothered to check what the rest of the letters were otherwise I might have noticed that they spelt Cardigan, which was nowhere near Swansea.

"Shall we stop and look at a map?" I suggested feeling dismayed. Jules pulled in and passed me the road atlas.

"I can't see with this stupid eye, the writing too small, you try," I passed it to her.

She peered at it, "Fuck!" she exclaimed, "I can't see without my reading glasses," and threw it back at me.

"I thought I was the one with the eye problems," I protested. I tried again, shutting my left eye and concentrating hard, using just my right eye. My left eye was useless anyway, and got us into this mess to start with.

As soon as I woke that morning and opened my eyes I was aware something was wrong. I tried to suppress my anxiety as I lay there opening and shutting them, comparing the sight between them. From the sound of crockery in the background, it was apparent that Jules was entering the breakfast phase of her morning routine. Since separating from our husbands Jules and I had lived together for nearly six months, and it still baffled me how she could spend an hour and a half getting ready for work.

On days when I was working up at the hospital I took me half an hour to shoot out the door, admittedly in a rather chaotic and unglamorous fashion. I guess that was the difference, Jules glided out looking cool and sophisticated, perhaps I could achieve to same look if I put more effort into my appearance?

This morning I only had a couple of private patients to see, and plenty time, but there were other things on my mind, chiefly my lack of vision, and I bumbled uncertainly into the kitchen and tried to revive myself with a cup of tea.

"Are you okay?" Jules asked me quizzically.

"I think there's something wrong with my eye," I said cautiously.

I'd only had my last operation twelve days previously and although my consultant had said my retinae could detach again I thought he was just being pessimistic. It had been three months since my first detachment, when I had an operation to fill my eye with oil and press the retinae flat again. This had been followed up with some laser treatment and then at the end of November I'd had another operation to take the oil out and fill the space up with gas.

The gas had gradually seeped out over following week, and as the level had gone down, a strange wobbly bubble had developed, which was like trying to look through a spirit level. It had been of great relief when a few days ago when this had finally gone and I had got a little bit of sight back, however, this morning I could see a shadow coming across it, surely it hadn't detached again?

"I'm not really sure what's wrong with it, it seems to depend which way I'm looking," I said, trying to find the best way of peering out of my left eye which made the shadow disappear.

"I'm going to work but let me know what's happening," Jules said firmly. "Right? If you need to go down to Swansea I can take you."

"Okay," I mumbled, not really wanting to think about the possibility. Jules left and shortly after I wandered down the road, to see my patients. I have to confess to not giving my full attention to them as I was preoccupied with my vision, and after the second patient had left I decided to ring my consultant down in Swansea and speak to him about my concerns.

"Well you better come down and we'll have a look at you," said Mr D. "The clinic closes at five."

"Okay I'll be there." It was normally about a three hour journey from where I lived and I always had to have someone prepared to go down with me and drive me back, because of the procedures affecting my eyes. My musical buddy, Jay, had accompanied me on my last four trips and was insured to drive my van. He'd used it to sleep in the hospital car park as he waited patiently for me for the couple of nights it had taken me to have my two previous operations, however there were problems with asking Jay, both economic and emotional.

Since I'd known him Jay had never had any money, in fact when I first met him he had been living in his workshop with few amenities, eking out a frugal existence repairing musical instruments. He had helped me learn to play the violin, accompanying me on his guitar and mandolin and sharing his musical knowledge with me. The intimacy of our music had drawn as close and we had shared many adventures together, our friendship helping me find the strength to walk away from married life.

Jay's ambitions had grown beyond his isolated existence in his workshop and he had found a mortgage company to lend him the money for a 'buy to let', buying his x-wife out of the house they jointly owned in the village of Dolwen. I had helped him convert it into a holiday let but there hadn't been enough business to make it profitable and eventually Jay had ended up living there with our friend, Jimmi, who was the bass player in our band Outlaw Jones. Between them they had scraped together enough money to pay the mortgage for the last three months, Jimmi used his benefits and Jay had sold everything he had acquired for the house to work as a holiday let.

Jay was down to his last few processions, hoping to get by until he was entitled to his state pension in February. He had acquired a car, swapping a guitar for it, but I knew he didn't have enough money to put petrol in the tank to get to my house, and, even if he managed to borrow some cash, there were the complications of our relationship to deal with when he arrived.

I loved Jay as a friend and musical partner, but didn't want a closer attachment; Jay did, and tended to be rather emotionally labile when he was around me. The complexities of our relationship had been added to with my recent hospital visits, which had made me more vulnerable and reliant on him. Weighing up the potential difficulties of asking Jay I decided to take Jules up on her offer, besides it should be a lot quicker using her car rather than taking my van. I texted her and she arrived home shortly afterwards.

"Do you want beetroot?" Jules said disappearing into the fridge.

"What?" The only thing on my list of essentials to take to hospital was my violin.

"I'm making you a packed lunch; I've already got mine from work. What do you want in it?"

"I don't know… anything." I couldn't think about food while I was distracted by the unpleasant possibility of having another eye operation so close to the last one. I had the two previous operations under local anaesthetic, each time spending more than an hour and a half on the operating table, and my courage was wearing a bit thin.

"Feta cheese?"

It was no wonder I called Jules "Crazy", a chalky, white lump of cheese hovered briefly in my thoughts, together with the long needle Mr D had stuck in my eye socket during my last operation.

"Actually, I don't think I want any lunch."

"You will in a couple of hours," Jules insisted, she was an irresistible force when she thought something was good for you.

"Just do what you think," I said trying to get her off my case. Jules disappeared back into the fridge, satisfied in her pursuit of a nourishing packed lunch, while I continued to chase my unpleasant thoughts around my head.

At last we were ready and left with plenty of time to get to Swansea, had the journey gone according to plan, however due to our unexpected tour of West of Wales, time was beginning to run out. I tried to focus more closely on the detail of the map with my good eye, "I think if we take this minor road and turn right at the next village we can make our way cross country towards Swansea. It's got to be quicker than going all the way round the coast."

Jules concurred with my analysis and as we made our way haphazardly across the Cardigan countryside we both agreed that the pretty rural villages would be a lovely place to stop for a pub lunch, if it weren't for the fact we were trying to make a hospital deadline. It was late afternoon by the time we pulled up into Singleton hospital car park and immediately we were both compelled to make a dash for the ladies toilets in the entrance lobby. I pushed open the door,

"What the fuck!" Jules gagged, as a toxic gas wafted out to greet us.

Both of us collapsed into hysterical laughter, partly due to the tension of the journey, but also because I knew how fastidious Jules was about public toilets and her present necessity meant she was about to meet her nemesis. There were two cubicles, one occupied, and I forged on ahead into the free one, leaving Jules to face the possible perpetrator of the smell behind the locked door. I heard toilet flush and a muttered apology as the phantom pong maker made a fast exit. Neither, Jules, or I, wanted to hang around either and as soon as we had finished our ablutions we both rushed out to escape the fetid air.

We made our way to the ophthalmology department in fits of giggles, Jules still trying to tell me about her disconcerting encounter with the lady behind the door as she had squeezed out the cubicle. Reaching the reception desk I checked in with the administrator and as we stood by the counter awaiting instructions, Jules suddenly froze in horror.

"That's the woman I met coming out of the toilet," she hissed nodding towards a large lady sitting in the reception area. The potential embarrassment of sitting next to the unfortunate woman set us off into hysterics again. Unfortunately toilet humour can be very debilitating and we were both rendered incapable of any further sensible conversation, I was vibrating with suppressed mirth while Jules spluttered every time she tried to talk. The administrator waved us further down the corridor to a deserted bay; clearly she had decided we were a danger to the normal people sitting quietly waiting for their appointments.

Forty five minutes later things didn't seem so funny and it was beginning to feel like we were doing time outside the Headmasters office for our indiscretions in the public conveniences. It reminded me of an occasion at primary school when, as a bored infant waiting in the dinner cue, I squirted water from a drinking fountain up the wall, to see how high it would go, and was caught by a monitor. I had to spend the whole lunch hour sitting crossed legged by the teachers table while they ate their food and discussed my fate.

My punishment had been to spend the rest of the afternoon doing lines, copying "I must not play with water" over and over again, until I filled the page with my shaky six year old writing. I had been given a sheet of plain paper and as I looked back up the page to repeat my pencilled efforts I realised to my horror that each line sloped down the page a little more than the last. My last few lines ended taking a convenient diagonal down to the bottom corner of the page, reaching it short of the many repetitions I would have had to have done, had my lines been straight.

It was a genuine error, rather than an attempt to curtail my penance, but my experience of teachers was that they tended to be fickle creatures, not usually empathetic towards children's mistakes. Fortunately it was the end of the day and the teacher was bored of torturing me so allowed me to go home with the rest of the class. Returning to my present situation I wondered whether I would be so lucky again and if Mr D would allow me to leave and go home with Jules.

Eventually a nurse ushered me through a door and I was greeted by a doctor I'd never seen before, who starred intently into my eye while I rested my chin and forehead on the frame on top of the desk.

"Look past my left ear, up and left, down and left, right, down and right, up and right…" The instructions went on and on, always confusing me since I don't know my right from my left.

"Yes, well it appears the retinae has detached again. I'll book you on to the ward for a possible emergency operation tomorrow."

In my desperation I wondered whether he really knew what he was talking about and when I might see someone I could trust.

"When am I going to see Mr D?"

"Oh I expect he'll be around tomorrow morning on his rounds."

The doctor turned away to fill in the paperwork required to admit me on to the ward and I stood there immobilised by the distress that was threatening to swamp me. I stared at his back for a short while, before I managed to gather myself and went back out into the deserted corridor. Everyone had gone home apart from Jules who was sitting head down, messaging on her phone.

"It's detached again. I've got to stay and have another operation, maybe tomorrow."

I felt choked by self-pity, Jules gave me I hug but we both knew she had to leave. We went back out to the car and I collected my stuff, then Jules drove away and I walked back to the hospital alone. I took the lift up to Ward Two.

"You back?" said a nurse.

"Unfortunately yes," I said despondently, it felt all too familiar. Then, as I was clerked in, something wonderful happened; I was shown into a single room all to myself. Suddenly things didn't seem quite as bad and I shut the door, unpacked my violin and started to play. Jay and I were going through a bit of an Irish phase. I started with the *Boat Song* and then went into *Buskers*

Fantasy and Morrison's Reel. The Celtic notes drifted into the corners of the sterile room, softening its edges, and pouring a cathartic balm on my troubled mind.

The first two songs had been taught to me by my violin teacher, Sarah, who I'd managed to have some lessons with before the latest debacle with my eye. Without being able to read music I had found it difficult to find a teacher I could relate to and was pretty much self-taught; however a chance encounter with Sarah had led to some very positive lessons which I hoped could continue once my eye was sorted.

Strangely Sarah had been in Swansea playing a gig when I'd been there for my last eye operation, and after I'd signed the necessary forms for my pre-op, I'd managed to escape from hospital and see her play that evening,. That had been less than two weeks ago, but now without Sarah, or the trusty Jay, it looked like the entertainment was down to me.

After playing for a while I relaxed and even felt a bit hungry, blessing Crazy for the oversized lunch she had packed me, which was large enough for supper as well. I wouldn't be having anything to eat or drink after midnight as the nurse had said I might be having the operation tomorrow and this time I had decided to have a general anaesthetic, rather than a local. The injections for my last operation had been quite uncomfortable and the whole procedure a slightly alarming and protracted affair, as I found I could watch the operation happening inside the affected eye, which had been frozen and clamped open.

I had made the discovery as I lay on my back on the operating table and tried to distract myself from the boredom and claustrophobia of staring at the blue sheet over my face by looking out of the eye being operated on. Much to my surprise and intrigue, I could see the sharp instruments being used as they poked around inside it. As I watched Mr D had squirted some dye in, which mixed psychedelically with some oil droplets, before he sucked the mixture up a pipette, the droplets making a pleasing orderly line. Next the black silhouette of a pair of forceps entered the fray, which he used to try and delicately peel back the scar tissue that had formed over my retinae since he had done the first operation.

"I can see your forceps," I informed him, thinking he might be interested.

Mr D made a slightly surprised noise, which I wasn't sure whether was from shock, or just that I had disturbed his concentration. He wasn't having much luck picking up the thin membrane and the forceps kept dabbing back for another attempt. I focused on the forceps, willing him to make a strike.

"You've got it!" I said congratulating him as he lifted it. Mr D faltered and nearly dropped it. I decided it might be best to keep quiet for the rest of the operation and cheered him on silently as he peeled back the scar tissue in tiny little pieces and popped in a new plastic lens to replace my damaged one.

Well it had been an interesting experience but maybe I would give it a miss this time around and accept the offer of sleeping though it. I wondered how Crazy was getting on as she made her way haphazardly across the Welsh countryside, she must be exhausted. I imagined without navigation aids her route might be similar to one taken by the ball in pinball machine, good job her new love, Seb, was at the other end to collect the pieces. Their relationship was complex, so far it had been a rollercoaster ride, and was the reason I called her Crazy, but Jules was convinced he was the man for her and was patiently waiting for Seb to realise that she was the woman for him.

Once Seb texted me that Jules had arrived back safely I decided to get ready for bed and realised in the chaos of leaving home I had packed six pairs of socks but only one pair of pants. I washed the ones I had on, hung them on the radiator, and visited the bathroom. My room was almost on-suite, with a toilet right next to my room and I felt very lucky with my relative privacy from other patients. At 2 am I decided to visit 'my' toilet again and was slightly put out when I found another patient sitting on it. She was attached to a mobile drip and slumped forward. She looked up at me as I entered, "I just want to die," she groaned.

I thought about asking her if she could find another place to plan her demise, her timing was very inconvenient, but in the end decided to seek assistance and went to inform the nurses at their night station.

"There's a lady in the toilet outside my room who seems a bit distressed."

"Oh, is she still there?" clucked a nurse.

Two of them returned with me and opened the toilet door and we all stared at the lady who was still in the same repost.

"I just want to die," repeated the lady.

"Now come along, don't be so silly," tutted the nurses as they dragged her off the toilet and wheeled her away with her drip.

I watched them go and turned back to look at the empty toilet; suddenly I had lost the urge and went back to bed.

I got a little sleep before the early morning round of taking blood pressure and temperatures started, this was followed by breakfast but there was nothing for me. I wondered when I would see Mr D and when I would have my operation. I turned away the tea trolley and waited, occasionally picking up my violin but my heart wasn't in it, the uncertainty of my situation was too distracting. The morning dragged on and I went out three times to ask for updates at the nurse's station. They sympathised with my predicament and made phone calls, but nobody knew.

The lunch trolley came. I was hungry, but most of all thirsty, yesterday evenings cup of tea seemed a long time ago, I might continue to starve all afternoon and still not have an operation today. There seemed no point in waiting any longer and I had just finished a packet of sandwiches and a drink when Mr D's registrar rocked up in his theatre gown.

"Sorry, been in theatre all morning. You can go on the emergency list this evening, but you will have to have a local anaesthetic now you've eaten."

"Well I don't particularly want another local but I don't want to wait until tomorrow either, so let's do it." I signed the consent form he put in front of me and waited for the afternoon to pass. Once the nurses started squirted the dilating drops in my eye I knew that count down had begun; by tea time I was putting on my gown, then the porter came with his trolley, covered me with a blanket and wheeled me down the corridor.

I found the sequence of events gradually stripped me of my autonomy and built up the suspense of the operation, and when I arrived in the preparation area outside the theatre I realised how nervous I was. The nurse offered me her hand and Mr D suddenly appeared in close up; his needle coming straight towards me.

I think the nurse regretted giving me her hand as I crushed in proportion to the pain of the needle being pushed into my eye socket. It can't have been any worse than when I'd had my first operation, but the last twenty four hours of stress seemed to be concentrated on the point of the needle. Normally the second injection wasn't as bad, however the anaesthetic from the first one still hadn't taken effect and tears of distress squeezed out of the corners of my eyes. By the time my eye was numb I felt shattered and the rest of the operation passed in a haze of grey shadows.

The following morning Jay turned up to rescue me. He borrowed some money off Jimmi and managed to put enough petrol in the tank to get to Swansea. It was good to see him but I was also uneasy. While it was wonderful having someone who cherished me it was also felt like a heavy burden because I couldn't return the favour. He was going through one of his "I understand how you feel," phases and "It's cool just to be friends." Unfortunately these never lasted very long before he became moody and upset and say that he couldn't cope being around me. The trouble was neither of us seemed very good at staying away from each other and the cycle would begin all over again.

It took ages to leave the hospital because pharmacy was so slow doing their rounds. After two hours we gave up and left without my eye-drops, I had plenty at home anyway. I was sore, tired and ratty and when we arrived back I argued with Jay, I can't even remember about what, and he left cross. After he had gone I noticed a large oil slick running down the steep road outside my house where he had been parked, evidence of a leak in his tank. Everything seemed as dismal as the black mess that dripped down the drain. I sighed, exasperated, and went inside. It was only two weeks to Christmas and I certainly wasn't feeling very festive.

It would be the first Christmas since I'd separated from my husband and I didn't really care what I did as long as my children were happy with arrangements. They decided they would have a late breakfast with me and open their presents and then have dinner with their Dad. Jay and Jimmi had invited me to have dinner with them and I was looking forward to relaxing from the tensions of a family Christmas, however there was still a bit of turmoil to get through with Crazy Jules before I could chill.

It was the night before Christmas and nothing stirred except… Seb had left stockings outside the house for me and Jules. I knew Jules was disappointed, she had hoped to spend Christmas Eve with him and even though she was going to spend the following day with him it wasn't the night she had planned.

"Let's open our presents to each other now," she said with forced gaiety.

"Okay," I said warily.

I wasn't sure that the old Duran Duran hit album, I had found in the Red Cross shop, was going to make her laugh at this point in time, or whether she would see the funny side of the apron with 'Master Chief' written on it, in reference to her reluctance to do any cooking since she had left her husband, nonetheless as the wrapping paper got strewn around the floor she cheered up a bit.

"Let's watch Oliver Twist," she said suggested, still determined to have a good time. The DVD had been another 'brilliant' idea of mine, knowing how much Jules loved musicals, but I hadn't been planning on spending Christmas Eve watching it. Well, I guess there are worse things to do than sing your way through Lionel Bart's timeless songs with your crazy house-mate, but hopefully tomorrow would be less strained and Jules would be with the person she really wanted to be with. Watching Jules going through the emotional stress of having someone special in her life was a useful reminder to me of how debilitating love could be. It was not something I felt I wanted or needed, especially when music and writing took so much of my energy.

More present opening followed the next day, firstly with my children and Jules's grown up daughter, Tamsin. There were various competitions to see who got the weirdest and most tasteless present, with quite a few contenders, before Jules finally went to Seb's house and I went to Dolwen to see Jay and Jimmi. The guys had gone to town with the festivities and it made me feel special. Jay had made miles of paper chains and they hung from the high ceilings, occasionally falling down with a gentle rustle of paper as the glue dried out. As it was Christmas the wood stoves were lit both in the kitchen and the lounge, much to my relief, as it was usually freezing unless you stayed within a couple of feet of the kitchen fire. Jimmi, who loved cooking, roasted a large chicken, with all the trimmings, especially lots of stuffing which was his favourite. We played some music, watched some TV and the time passed pleasantly as it does when you're with good friends.

I stayed with them again over New Year and we lit sparklers to welcome 2014, it took very little to amuse me, it was just a relief to pause after the previous year's frenetic activity. During 2013 I toiled for months to help Jay with his holiday home business and move his belongings around the Welsh countryside, separated from my husband, left the family home and decorated and furnished my own house, had a house mate move in with me, juggled my relationships with my children, responsibilities as a mother and various guilt trips, carried on with work and running through various injuries, had two retinal detachments and three operations on my eye, finished writing my first book, and with the help of Jay and Jimmi, recorded my first album. I hoped in 2014 my retinae would stop detaching and I would get my book and CD published, then I would be satisfied... or would I?

Chapter 2. Sore Brain

Her head felt like elephants were doing the merengue on her cerebellum. (Susan Fanetti)

The year started pleasantly enough with Jimmi's Scouse mate, Muttley, turning up and staying for a short holiday in Dolwen. They were old friends who had grown up together in Liverpool and spent most of their time laughing and exchanging gags, mixing music for Muttley's Jazz project, and going out for walks, taking pictures of the local scenery.

"Can I have a look at your pictures," I asked Muttley as he returned with Jimmi from another trip, his camera hanging around his neck.

He passed it to me and I started to flick through dozens of pictures. Trees, rivers and barb wire, hills, fields and barb wire, sheep and barb wire, fences, walls and more barb wire.

"Hey Muttley, what's with all the barb wire?" I asked him puzzled.

"Reminds me of home," he sniggered.

I laughed. Scousers!

Eventually Muttley went and it was time to go back down to Swansea again for another eye check-up. Although only a day trip, Jay offered to take me in the van, because you never knew about these things. The journey down there proved straight forward and the check-up brief; all was well with my eye, the retina flat and pressure normal, and it wasn't very long until we were on our way back home again. The main road, leading out of Swansea soon gave way to the narrow rural lanes that weave randomly across Ceredigion. It was dark and misty night and the wind screen wipers swished back and forwards as the headlight strained to penetrate the blackness.

"The warning lights come on," said Jay suddenly.

"What does that mean?" I asked looking at the red light on the control panel.

"I'm not sure but the engine's over-heating and we need to stop," and in saying so he switched off the engine. We had stopped in a dark hedged lane, somewhere between Carmarthen and Aberystwyth, with no mobile reception.

"You can't just stop here if another vehicle comes by they'll hit us. Look there's a drive way, lets pull in there," I suggested pointing to an entrance on the right.

Jay parked in front of the modern built house and got out and lifted the bonnet of the van. He re-appeared a short while later with the results of his investigation.

"Looks like the fan belts gone; we can't really go any further. We'll have to see if they mind us parking here."

"I'll go, I look less scary than you," I said jumping out.

I knocked on the door but there was no reply. Walking down the outside of the building I noticed a dim light from one of the windows and peered inside. Two men were sitting at a table. I knocked on the window and they looked up suspiciously, I hadn't taken into account that although I could see in they couldn't see out. Reluctantly one of them came to the door and opened it a crack with the other man looking over his shoulder.

"Hi," I said brightly as I stood there in the pouring rain. I was tempted to say, "I come in peace," but bit my tongue. "We've broken down. Is it all right if we park in your driveway and can I use your phone to call a garage?"

There was a pause as the man thought about it.

"We don't have a phone," he said in doom laden Welsh accent.

His announcement took me back slightly, but only a little, it was not the first time I had knocked on a door at night in rural Wales, in search of a phone to be disappointed. When I was younger, long before mobile phones had been invented, I had been in charge of school group on an evening's caving trip. The van had broken down and I had left the other instructor in charge while I had gone in search of a phone to call the outdoor centre and ask them to come and rescue us. I had hitched a ride, convinced I would soon find help, but the only houses I found were either unoccupied or claimed to have no phones.

Eventually I had found a phone in a pub, miles away from the breakdown, and then had to wait there until closing time before I was collected. The fact that I was standing in a pub for two hours in a wetsuit, and no one commented on my attire, says a lot about how drunk everyone must have been. Well fast forward some years and here I was again standing in the rain outside a house with no phone and a broken down van. Only the wetsuit was missing.

The man opened the door a little wider, "If you go back down the road, about quarter of a mile, Evans the garage might be able to help you. There are a lot of four by fours on the road side, you can't miss it."

"Oh thanks," I said as the door quickly shut. I went back to Jay and relayed the information.

"I think I spotted it," he said, "we might as well check it out, it's not far."

A couple of minutes later I was standing outside another dimly lit house and went through the knocking on the door scenario again. This time a woman came to the door.

"Oh it's my husband you want," she said and disappeared calling to him. A man returned and listened to my tale.

"Well I can order you a fan belt on the supply van that comes by every morning from Carmarthen. Will you be alright staying in your van? There's a tap and outside toilet in the yard."

"Yes, thanks for your help," I said gratefully.

All things considered we had broken down in a pretty convenient spot with amenities to hand and garage able to get us a spare part. We just had to pass the night and wait for the fan belt to arrive. My van has a rock-and-roll bed in the back of it and I always carry bedding, so the sleeping arrangements were sorted, it was a cold night and the morning brought a confusion of emotions. Jay was looking bright and cheerful and we had just had some breakfast and were tidying up, when Mr Evans knocked on the van door to take a look at the engine and establish the size of fan belt he needed to order for us.

"The wife says come in for a cup of tea," he said as he put the bonnet down. We followed him back to the kitchen where Mrs Evans fussed over us with tea and cakes. She liked to talk, and since her six children had left home, and Mr Evans had carried on with the business long after his retirement age, I don't think she'd had much of an opportunity. Considering how isolated their house was there seemed to be a lot going on, but the only evidence of any people was the large chapel next door to the Evans's.

"Where do all the people come from to support the chapel?" I asked Mrs Evans who cleaned it.

"The farming community, they use to walk for miles across the fields to come to a service on a Sunday but now not many come," she sighed regretfully.

Mr Evans, who sat glowering in the corner, did not seem to have the same remorse about the absence of local farmers, whom he was convinced were worth millions but were reluctant to part with any of their money.

"If I had their subsidies I could have retired long ago, but you try and get them to pay you any money when you've done a job for them," he said crossly. His son in law, Glyn the mechanic, nodded in agreement while sipping his tea. Jay and I hastily made it clear that we were not related to any farmers and did not support the common agricultural policy, especially when it came to farming subsidies. Mrs Evans smiled and passed us some more cakes.

We decided to go and look round the chapel, which was a large impressive space built to resonate with the sound of Welsh voices joined in hymn. Now it was silent and the only people around were the dead ones in the graveyard, there were a lot of those judging from the wonky headstones. Inside the chapel Mrs Evans had put a bucket out to catch the drips from the leaking roof. There was a fund to fix it, although, to me, there seemed little point in preserving a building surrounded by dead people, which live people no longer used.

By the time we got back the fan belt had arrived, however when Glyn tried to fix it he had discovered the thingy that allowed the belt to rotate had rusted, and therefore we needed a new one of those too, or the belt would break again. Glyn scrabbled around all the broken vehicles in the yard, trying to cannibalise the part, but to no avail. All seemed lost until Mr Evans called the supply garage from Aberystwyth, which would be passing later that afternoon, and discovered that they could supply the required part.

We were saved and decided to leave the warm comfort of the kitchen and celebrate by playing some music in the van. We never went anywhere without out instruments and used them to do the talking between us. For a while it was just me a Jay playing music, and we shared an interesting exchange until the cold eventually drew us back into the kitchen for more tea and cakes. At last the part arrived, the van was fixed and we were on our way, gratefully waving goodbye to the very kind Mr and Mrs Evans. We seemed to go a different way every time we went to

Swansea but should we pass by again it was definitely a top spot to break down. By the time we got back it was 28 hours since we'd left Swansea and, although young, the New Year was already proving to be quite eventful.

…

My eye made me feel all unbalanced and weird, one side was normal while the other was oily and blurry. I had to go for a special eye test to prove that I was still safe to drive by sticking my head in a box and pressing a button every time a light appeared. I only missed a few in the bottom left hand quadrant, which was good enough to be fit to drive, however I didn't like driving before my retinae detached and now I liked it even less. I found manoeuvring in traffic, pulling out of junctions and reversing, particularly worrying, my problems compounded by driving a wide transit van whose width I wasn't able to judge very well. I hoped my next operation might bring some improvements and looked forward to the date in February with mixed emotions.

The day before my operation was due I decided to go out for a run; it might be my last chance for a while. I loved to run along the beach and clear my mind but it had become trickier since my eye problems as I couldn't judge the ground very well and sometimes stumbled over the rippling sand. On this occasion I came back across the golf course and a Jack Russell raced up behind me yapping aggressively. I heard the owner call and the dog hesitated, I decided to carry on, thinking it had turned back, I realised my mistake as I felt a sharp pain in my calf and a worried shout from the owner. The dog retreated and I continued, reluctant to stop and record a slower time on the phone app I was using. I got back to the house, stopped my timer and then peeled back my tracksuit bottoms to examine the damage. The dog bite had broken the skin and blood trickled down the muscle.

I gave Crazy a text to report my latest misfortune, she replied, *"When did you last have a tetanus injection?"* I couldn't remember and decided I'd best go to the local hospital and get one, rather than go for my eye operation with the added complication of lock jaw. The duty nurse cheerfully stabbed me in the arm while telling me a gruesome tale of how her daughter had been bitten by a dog and ended up with such a bad infection that she needed intravenous antibiotics.

"Watch out for streaks of infection going up the leg," she said darkly as I left.

I got back to house and was half way through regaling Crazy with my tale when she gave me a nudge. The owner of the dog was coming up the garden path with a bunch of flowers. He was so apologetic I didn't like to tell him that tulips were not my favourite and really I was fine, I loved dogs when they weren't attacking me.

When Jay came to pick me the next day, the weather forecasters were promising dire things. It was the winter of the great storms and Aberystwyth had already been beaten to a pulp by raging seas, but worse things were to come that day, with winds of 100mph. Things weren't too bad when we left, but the winds got stronger as we approached Swansea, overhead power lines swinging like skipping ropes while the van was buffeted by such powerful winds against its high sides that it threatened to topple over. Jay fought with the steering wheel to keep us from being pushed across the road and we managed to keep ahead of the trees that were falling down behind us, only discovering their sawn remains on our return journey.

I signed in and had the usual tests, then returned to the van to have my last supper with Jay before my general anaesthetic the following day. I was glad to be spending the night in the hospital as I left Jay to be 'gently' rocked to sleep in the swaying van while the wind screamed him a lullaby, whipping through the pipes and gaps of one of the nearby buildings. I was back in a bed on a shared ward again, but it was a lot quieter than being in the storm that raged outside, despite the bubbling nebulisers attached to two of the patients.

At 6am I was given a small bowl of cornflakes to sustain me until my operation sometime in the afternoon. The morning passed quickly as I watched the entertainment provided by the patients and staff around me. One lady was complaining of chest pain and a throng of nurses gathered around her. Their collective wisdom was that she was having an angina attack and that a higher authority, in the form of a doctor, should be called to deal with the problem. By the time the doctor appeared, twenty minutes later, her chest pains had gone, however I was now more concerned by the lady in the opposite bed whose nebuliser had run out and I hadn't seen move since. More doctors appeared, but they were only interested in interrogating the lady with the chest pains, one kneeling at the foot of her bed looking as if he was praying; perhaps Western medicine took a more spiritual approach these days?

Meanwhile a nurse snapped the elasticated oxygen mask off the apparently dead patient in the opposite bed and I saw her move and open her eyes. Phew, she was only asleep. The doctors finally left the room, the excitement was over, and it wasn't long before I was wheeled away on my trolley and put to sleep myself. After what seemed like moments later I woke up in recovery and was soon back on the ward. To my surprise I felt alright, even feeling like I could tackle the strange looking green hospital jelly with the film of bubbles on top of it…or perhaps not. Jay came to visit me and once he had left I decided it was time to go to the bathroom. As I sat there I suddenly felt that all was not right with the world and could feel myself breaking out into a cold sweat, with the promise that a rising tide of vomit was on its way.

I managed to get off the toilet and open the door but couldn't get any further and clutched on to the sink for support. Fortunately the nurses were doing their rounds and a couple of them rushed to my rescue, but there was no way I was letting go of the sink. My body was racked by spasms of retching and as my head jerked forward I was in danger of knocking myself out on the tap.

"You must let go of the sink Jess," said one nurse as she prised my fingers from the porcelain and threw me back onto the commode that the other nurse was holding. My feeble resistance didn't really stand a chance; they'd obviously done the 'Breakaway' course similar to the one I'd taken once, during an annual round of NHS mandatory training that all employees endured. I didn't remember being taught a procedure on how to release the hands of a patient intent of holding on to inanimate objects, only a technique to free me from the clutches of any patient that might choose to strangle me, but working in the NHS you have to be prepared for all kinds of scenarios. It was actually a wonder that I had retained any information from that particular course as my thoughts were more on Harriet the Hamster…

Ben's hamster, Harriet, had come on her summer holidays to stay with my son. She was in temporary residence in his bedroom but as another little boy was coming for a sleep over so I decided to move her cage down into the utility to make more space. I put the cage down gently and peered in, Harriet was curled up fast asleep in her hay, a cute little bundle of fluff. I looked closer; suddenly concerned that I couldn't see any signs indicating she was breathing. Feeling alarmed I quickly opened the cage door and lifted her from her nest, the small body lay unresponsive in the same position. She was dead.

"Are you sure she's dead?" said my husband.

Even if I hadn't been a medical professional for years I was sure I could spot a dead hamster, what did he think; she was hibernating in the middle of July? I felt a sense of panic, there were two small boys upstairs expecting to play with Harriet, and one young boy due back from holiday expecting to see his pet. I couldn't bear to disappoint any of them, if I could find a substitute hamster none of them need find out. There was only one problem, the next day was a mandatory training day and I was supposed to be doing Breakaway training, 'operation Harriet' would have to be planned carefully to continue the illusion that all was well until I could find a replacement.

The following day I gave strict instructions to my son that he was not to disturb Harriet because she was very tired and needed to sleep all day. I left the house on a mission and as soon as we were given a coffee break, from the self-defence course, I got my mobile out and phoned the pet shop in Aberystwyth.

"Hi do you have any hamsters in stock?… Great! It needs to be a brown one with white patches… What's an Abyssinian one look like?...No, it has to have short hair… Sort of hamster sized…No it was round, not pointy…Little ears…A What?

After a long and frustrating conversation it didn't sound like the pet shop had anything that looked like Harriet, I had no idea there were so many kinds of hamster. During the lunch break I tried Newtown pet shop with better results and as soon as the course finished that afternoon I set off to find Harriet mark 2 before the shop closed. The shop keeper's instructions led me to a car park, where I realised I didn't have any change for the metre. It would have to be a quick raid before a car-park attendant came round and I got clamped, I flew into the shop.

"Hi I phoned earlier, you've got some brown and white hamsters?"

"Yes over there," the lady directed me to a cage full of Harriet look-a-likes.

"Great that one will do," I pointed to one which seemed to have the same patches as Harriet. The lady scooped it out and put it in a small cardboard box with some straw.

"It will eat its way out of this in about half an hour," she warned.

I looked at her aghast, "It's about an hour back home, what am I going to do?"

I had a horrid vision of Harriet mark 2 escaping from her box and doing wall of death around the interior of the car causing me to have a fatal crash. I explained my dilemma to the pet shop owner and the importance of bringing back a replacement hamster.

"Have you cleaned out the old cage yet?"

"No, because I needed to leave the dead hamster pretending to be alive until I got another one."

"Well, you need to replace all the bedding because the smell of the other hamster will send this one mad. Also it will take time to get it used to being handled; it may well bite the new owner if he's not careful."

I imagined Ben getting back from holiday to be savaged by Harriet mark 2, that was presuming I even managed to get her home. It was now apparent my brilliant plan was flawed on several levels. I would have to own up and come clean with the boys about Harriet's long and ostensibly peaceful sleep.

"Forget the hamster," I said hurriedly as I rushed out of the shop before I got done for parking. The return journey took twice as long as it should have done due to a diversion caused by an accident, maybe someone else had decided to risk taking a hamster for a long drive in a cardboard box. When I got back I messaged Sue, Ben's mum, about Harriet's unfortunate demise and put her in the freezer so she would look her best for Bens return. A few days later I took her defrosted body round for a ceremonial burial in a shady spot in Ben's garden. He gave her a small piece of apple to sustain her for the journey onwards into after-life and she left the world peacefully, unaware of the drama she had caused.

"Don't worry," said Sue, "she was quite old I was thinking she wouldn't live much longer. We won't be getting another they're far too much problem." I couldn't have agreed more and wondered if she would have blessed me if my subterfuge had worked and Harriet's astonishing longevity had broken all records for hamsters.

Back on the ward in Singleton hospital the nurse wheeled me back to my bed clutching a sick bowl. I was given an anti-sickness injection and my blood pressure was taken. Unfortunately because of the position of the bed against the wall they had to take it from the arm which had already had the tetanus injection in it, and my stiff muscles protested as the cuff remorselessly squeezed my systolic rates from them. This unpleasant pain kept reoccurring, as there is nothing that ward nurses like better than taking your blood pressure every two minutes. It was time to escape, and the following morning, as soon as my eye had been checked, Jay and I made our way back through the storm battered country so I could lick my wounds at home.

To try and stabilise the eye, and stop it detaching again, Mr D had inserted a silicon band into it. It seemed to have the desired effect but the down side was that it gave me thumping headaches, and I was constantly tired, very tired. Trying to adjust to the very different vision between my two eyes was disorientating, and I was forced to take it easy. While convalescing I decided it was the ideal opportunity to concentrate on finishing the project I'd been working on for the last couple of years. I had written a book about my adventures learning to play the violin, along with a CD that Jay and Jimmi had helped me produce, on which we played the music I had been writing about. It was time to publish the book and CD, it felt like a defining moment had arrived.

...

I stuck an eye patch on and tried to focus on the computer, but found it slow and tedious going through the book edits with one eye. Fortunately my friend Sue, of the afore mentioned hamster episode, painstakingly helped me go through all the typos and Jay did his bit too, but the missing commas and full-stops seemed endless and I realised at some stage I would have to call a halt and be happy with less than perfection.

I looked for a literary agent and bought a copy of the *Writers Year Book* to try and direct my book towards a suitable publisher. After half a dozen attempts I was disillusioned, no one apparently was looking for such a book or thought it commercially viable, I wasn't even sure if they'd read the short section I'd attached when trying to follow the various instructions for submission posted on the agents websites. I decided to self-publish an eBook on Kindle. Once you'd worked out how to format and upload it, publishing was a fairly instant process and at least with an eBook you didn't have to present a definite version, you could edit and upload corrections as many times as you wanted. More importantly it should work as the book I had envisaged, where the tap of finger linked you straight through to the music, enabling the reader to hear the music they had just read about.

While I tried to work out how to format the book for uploading, Jay concentrated on the music side of things. The recordings had been finished the previous autumn but I needed a website where the music could be played and downloaded to accompany the eBook, as well as a CD to accompany the hard copy of the book. Jay cleverly designed a website and uploaded the tracks, as well as finding a company that would produce CD's for a reasonable rate. He sent off Jimmi's master copy of the tracks, along with a cover he had created, and a week later a hundred CDs were posted to us. The picture we used on the front cover was a result of a photo shoot, one cold January afternoon, on a forestry track above the village of Dolwen, where Jay and Jimmi lived. We had put the instruments in the back of my van, wrapped up warmly and drove up through the forest until there was a good view over the hills, still trimmed with snow. Jimmi fixed his camera on a tripod, set the time delay and rushed to join me and Jay in the line out. If you look carefully on the picture you can see our teeth chattering.

With the music now ready it was time to commit to the latest version of the book and format and upload it. A couple of weeks of cerebral melt down as I tried to do follow the instructions on the Kindle site; "I can't do it," my brain continually screamed at me, only desisting from its chants when I lay down on the floor beating it in frustration. Later, when I thought the panic centre of my brain didn't notice, I would creep back to the computer and try to go through things logically, until I became overwhelmed again and slumped back on the floor in hopelessness. It was in one of these moments of despair that I finally had a brain wave; I would look on You Tube for a 'How to format and upload a book for Kindle', instructional video.

I tapped in the search and there they were, loads of videos, dead easy to follow with the computer screen pictured and which buttons to press. Simples! The hardest part was uploading the picture for the book cover, which fortunately Jay helped me with. We had taken a picture of my five string violin on the kitchen table at Dolwen, together with Jimmi's scarf and Jay's hat, but it had to fit into a template, which proved complicated. Eventually Jay sorted it and on the 1st March my eBook was published on Amazon, combining the two expressions of writing and music. It had taken me two years to write the book and four years to learn to play the violin and play the music on the accompanying CD.

Individually I thought they were entertaining, but together they complemented each other, enhancing the experience for the reader and listener. It turned out that using Amazon's Create Space; I could also publish a hard copy of the book, which would be printed on demand. This couldn't be changed once you had committed to a print version, but by April I had taken that step and was amazed at the size of the book I finally held in my hand as a testament to my accomplishments. 133,000 words seemed to weigh quite a lot and goodness knows how many musical notes there were on the slim CD that went with it. Of course without Jay and Jimmi the story would have been different and the notes not recorded. I was never going to be a great violinist, but together we had made something really good, music that had a happy vibe, and that played the music of my soul.

As far as I was aware the concept of an E book illustrated by music was a unique idea. I wanted other people to share it my experience, and to read and listen to it, but how was I going to do that? After you'd plucked up the courage to tell friends and family what then? And would friends and family be that interested anyway, or appreciate the effort and courage it had taken me to achieve it?

Chapter 3. Sore Fingers

The single biggest problem in communication is the illusion that it has taken place. (George Bernard Shaw)

For the moment I wasn't brave enough to admit to any family members that I'd written a book, especially when that book was about me and revealed a whole different life none of them were aware of. I decided to approach friends and acquaintances first and see what they thought of it. I suppose I was looking for some acknowledgement that I had done a good piece of work, that my writing was witty and interesting and my music entertaining.

The reactions to my announcement, by email or face to face, were usually one of enthusiasm and even admiration of my achievement, often followed by a lack of action when it actually came to reading or listening. A follow up enquiry would be usually answered with "I've been too busy."

I felt down hearted. I had laid myself open to judgement, as far as I dared, in fact one friend expressed surprise that she couldn't believe someone as private as me had written about events I'd never spoken to anyone about. I tried reason with myself that I couldn't expect people to be as fascinated with my project as I was, however if I couldn't get people who knew me to be interested, then who would be ? What about musicians? It was that time of year when my thoughts turned to Sore Fingers and whether circumstances and finances might allow me to go to this American roots music camp during the Easter break, maybe the people there might be curious about my musical tale.

I managed to book a place on the fiddle course and armed with some hard copies of the book and CD's, set off for Chipping Norton. Jay was coming with me for the first time to check out the Dobro class and was excited by the prospect of us spending some time together. The previous week he had come with me for another eye check-up, fortunately this time in Aberystwyth, closer to home. I had the usual eye test before I went through to the consulting room where I saw Mr B, who had originally referred me to Swansea; he was looking at my results when I walked in.

"It's amazing you can see anything after four operations, Mr D has done a fantastic job in the circumstances. I shall write and tell him," he said enthusiastically.

I didn't like to tell him about the problems it was causing me when trying to focus, instead I rested my chin on the frame and Mr B stared intently into my eye.

"Hmmm it's a bit juicy," he said, "but that's what you'd expect, it's a sick eye."

"Juicy?" I thought, not a medical term I was familiar with, but described quite well what it felt like. Oh well, I guess I'd get used to it.

After the appointment Jay and I went to the seafront, in the van, and sat with the side door open watching the world go by. It had been the perfect evening, some bread, cheese and wine and then playing music with your best friend while the sun went down. The feeling of harmony between us was a rare moment these days since my check-up in January when the van had broken down. Now as the music flowed I think Jay hoped the moment might last, but that's what it was, a moment. I pushed the worry of his expectations to the back of my mind and hoped that the music would take over his priorities once we arrived at Sore Fingers.

We drove down with the aid of Seb's Sat Nav, Jane. The former holder of the post, Doris, had been permanently retired, she had become very eccentric and petulant, often refusing to turn up for work, and I had decided it was time to part-company. Jane was proving to be quite competent but was accompanied by a crazed mooing noise every time I went over the speed limit, causing me to jump as I looked out for the manic animal crossing the road.

"Please can you turn the cow off," I pleaded with Jay. The driving was starting to get to me and a mad cow wasn't helping.

Jay twiddled with Sat Nav settings.

"Would you prefer sheep or a cuckoo?" he asked calmly.

"I'll try the cuckoo."

"Would you like to try Tim instead of Jane?" he piped up a few minutes later.

Jay was finding all sorts of options on the control panel and suddenly a calm, assuring, male voice came from the speaker, and although ever so slightly patronising, Tim sounded more assertive than Jane.

"Okay, Tim and the cuckoo get my vote but we need to swap places, I can't drive in this traffic anymore, its freaking me out." Somehow in between changing animal noises on the Sat Nav we had gone off route and were now heading towards the middle of Wolverhampton. I pulled over and got in the passenger seat, although I was never sure if this was a better option than driving. As I sat there my visual disturbances made it seem like we were frequently in danger of crashing into obstacles on the left hand side of the vehicle. This, together with Jay's alarming habit of turning the steering wheel in the same direction of where ever he was looking, had me continually flinching and drawing in sharp breaths of alarm as we drove along.

It was a relief when at last we swept up the long drive of the boarding school grounds, taken over by Sore Fingers for the week, and Tim grandly announced "You have reached your destination." Jay would be camping behind the long austere building of Top School, which dominated the rise, along with the rest of the campers. As I helped unload his stuff and lug it into the field, Jay immediately identified a problem.

"Where are you going to be in the van?"

"Down at the tennis courts, I told you."

"Yes, but its miles away."

"Well, a couple of minutes."

Jay was not happy but there was no way round it and I left him muttering as I took the van down to where the distant sports courts lay. No snow drifts this year but the sunny weather and clear skies meant the nights were still cold. I put the kettle on and a disgruntled Jay joined me for tea.

"What's the matter?" I asked him.

"I thought we'd be a lot closer together that's all" (I think this was a double entendre that went beyond his camping circumstances). "I haven't really come set up for camping, as I assumed the van would be nearby and I could use it like I normally do. I haven't got anything to sit on and I forgot my ground sheet so everything is piled into the inner tent and it's really uncomfortable."

"Are you warm enough?"

"Yes I've got my double duvet."

"You're going to need more than that; it's really cold at night. Here, you can have this heavy blanket, which should help a bit." I dragged the blanket off the back seat and Jay shrugged his shoulders in a resigned way and took the blanket from me, disinterested in the warmth it might provide him.

"Thanks," he said nonplussed and might as well have said, "Thanks for nothing." We both obviously had a completely different outlook on the week and although I tried to jolly him along and cooked a meal, he remained disappointed with the way things were turning out. I was relieved when he went back to his tent for the night. We were on different wave lengths; I was here for one thing only, the music.

The next morning I went along to morning assembly, with two hundred plus other students, for the John and Moira show. I don't think John had changed his hairstyle since the sixties and this together with his drooping moustache and large stomach made it look it look like a despondent walrus was reading the pages of rules in front of us. Moira was doing her best school mam impression, interrupting and repeating a number of the walrus's instructions, while the lighting man was entertaining us with suitable illuminations on the stage behind that wittily accompanied the list of regulations.

The new improved "shortened" assembly format meant we only overran by fifteen minutes and we all trundled off as soon as it was over, carrying our various shaped instrument cases, to meet our new class mates in record time for a Sore Fingers first morning. My tutor, Brian, from the USA, was very enthusiastic and energetic, to the point where I wondered if he had too many blue sweets in his diet. We went round the circle introducing ourselves. I spotted Sandy, from the first time I had been to Sore Fingers, who had leapt off her bed to greet me so brightly when I entered the dormitory room a few years back. The rest of the group were all new to me and there were the usual scattering of nationalities, Irish, French, German, and American, amongst the Brits.

I didn't really take much notice of what anyone was saying as it was all along the same lines of "I have played the fiddle for "blah blah years" and this week want to get "blah, blah out of the course". Everyone seemed to be conforming to their national characteristics, Leo the cute young French man with his quaint accent, Harold, the serious sounding German, Diane, the friendly, bright American girl and Eimear, the Irish girl whose lilting voice surely meant she played her fiddle while her feet twirled around to River Dance.

As I pondered why Irish names were spelt so strangely, we reached the last man in the circle, John Paul, who seemed to be making himself as inconspicuous as possible, almost hiding behind Brian trying not to be noticed. He looked uncomfortable as he made his introduction and I was puzzled by his demeanour but cast it to the back of my mind as Brian started singing and playing the first song *I'm on my Way Back to the Old Home*.

I found singing and playing the fiddle at the same time very difficult, but Brian accomplished in with ease. It was quite a pleasant song except for the poor English at the end of the chorus which jolted me every time it was sung, "But there is no light in the window that shined long ago where I live." Would it been so hard to put it in the past tense, I wondered, or was the effect deliberate? Anyway it's amazing how such a simple song can be so complex and by the time we had learnt singing and fiddle harmonies, various kick offs and tags to start and finish it with, hammer-ons, slides, drones, double stops, accompanying chords and chops, I was already suffering information overload and it was only day one.

By Wednesday I had definitely peaked and it was a relief when we got to the end of the class and we finished off with Leo playing a classic Gypsy Jazz number *All of Me* as Brian gave him a master class.

"I'm sorry my tone is a little bit poopy," Leo apologised bashfully in his endearing French accent and we all burst out laughing. He sounded pretty good to me, like he was busking outside a café in the artist's quarter of Paris. Brian suggested he could make his interpretation a little more "dirty", like Stuff Smith. Leo made a good attempt of the famous black Jazz violinist's style and then class was over for the day.

I met up with Jay for some food and then we went up to Top School to await the evening's concert. We were early, so drifted around the corner of the building to watch the setting sun while having a quick play. Leo passed as we finishing Django Reinhardt's, *Nuages*, and then stopped to lay down on his back on the grassy bank in front of the school, looking at the sky. I sensed he wanted to play and called out to him to join us, which he quickly did.

We had a pleasant time playing a few jazz numbers and then switched to the Blues. Turned out Leo was a bit of a soul man too, as he smoked his way through *Sky is crying.* I wished that I'd started to play violin as young as Leo and had all that experience under my fingers. Still, I couldn't turn back the clock, and could only be the best that I could be from my own start point. On that note it was time to pack up and go into the evening concert.

The hall was packed for Bruce Molsky, an Old Time fiddling legend, and I guess a lot of the audience had seen him play on the Transatlantic Sessions with Aly Bain. Now, Bruce Molsky on TV was one thing, but Bruce Molsky live was something else.

His quiet, understated demeanour was deceptive as he had a charisma that dominated the stage. Although some of the other tutors did play with him, he didn't need them; he was a one man show. His voice was just right for those soulful Old Time tunes about loggers who had cut their hand off with a band saw and could no longer work, let alone play the fiddle, lost their love and were just waiting to die.

"Woman don't you weep for me. My hands can't fiddle and my heart's been broke… Lord and my time ain't long" he sang. Really, those old loggers were so melodramatic.

Later he moved on to faster, more cheering tunes and his bow began to flash across the strings, dipping and stroking the same notes over and over again, somehow building a bubble of sound around him, like he had some secret way of getting the notes to crash into each other and reverberate. The bubble extended out from him and hit me, like a blow to the chest, how did he do that? Another hero was born and Old Time music would never be the same again. We left the hall with the aura of Bruce still upon us and the notes of his fiddle filling the night skies.

Back in class Brian had a "great" idea. All the different instrumental groups would play *I'm on my Way Back to the Old Home* on the last day of the course, it would be "Awesome fun." There was little time to get excited by the prospect as we were about to spend the rest of the morning learning a hundred and one ways to play *Cripple Creek*. By now people were a bit more relaxed with each other and their personalities were coming out a bit more. The German gentleman was proving to have a sense of humour and John Paul was also making the odd quirky observation, even if he remained rather shy.

Brian was asked by one student what the difference was between a lick and a riff.

"I just tend to use them interchangeably as the same thing, I think," he frowned

"I think a lick is played as a one off part of a solo whereas a riff is repeated." John Paul said, sounding a little bit embarrassed.

"So you mean it's like a groove?" I asked interested

"Well, a riff can become a groove," he nodded

I remained intrigued by John Paul. Earlier, in a break, Diane had been asking him whether he had been to some of the festivals that she had been to in the States. He said that he had when touring with a couple of different bands, that I'd vaguely heard of, and told her was touring in the summer with Gillian Welch and Dave Rawlings. I was a bit of fan of theirs and had watched them on YouTube playing *Caleb Meyer* dozens of times. As one visitor to the site commented "Dave Rawlings is cooler than the other side of the pillow" and Gillian Welch was too, so I knew that John Paul must be special if he was touring with them.

Later when John Paul was examining the pegs on my fiddle I asked him what he normally played and he replied "Bass guitar and mandolin." I reckoned he must be pretty good on them, however he had more immediate problems with tuning his present instrument and examined the geared pegs I had on my five string fiddle, which made tuning so easy for me.

"I'd really recommend them," I said.

"I've noticed that a lot of violin player seem to adjust their fine tuners all the time."

"Yes. I've noticed that too, but actually I find that this hardly ever goes out of tune, which may be due to only having the string pulled at one end, rather than both ends like fine tuners do."

"I think I might try them," he said nearly convinced after I showed him how easy they were to adjust.

Harold had also taken notes of my make of shoulder rest, which he found much more secure than his own. Perhaps I should be a salesperson for violin parts; it seemed to be much easier to get enthusiastic about that than recommending either my book or CD. Admitting I'd written a book sounded pretentious and although Mel, Phil and Neil, from the scratch band that I'd previously played with at Sore Fingers, had all happily bought copies, other than them I had only shared my shameful secret with three other class mates: Sandy, because she made a brief appearance in chapter two, Tim, who I was sitting next to, and the approachable Dinah, who had immediately downloaded a copy. I had given a copy of the book and CD to our tutor, Brian, in the hope he might give me some feedback by the end of the week, even daring to hope he might allude to it in class, but he said nothing. I guess he was too busy organising all sorts of other things.

The week had flown by and suddenly it was the final morning. Brian led a couple of "Psycho" raids on the banjo classes which involved eighteen fiddlers running into the class and playing the screeching riff from the notorious stabbing in the shower scene of that film, before running out again. It was probably enough to give anyone nightmares for years to come, but fortunately in the afternoon there was the "awesome fun" of the whole of Sore Fingers playing *I'm on my Way Back to the Old Home* to help recover from the trauma.

Brian had us all lined up on the grassy bank in front of Top School, fiddlers, banjos, guitars, double bass players, all stood in their respective groups (I can't remember whether the autoharps were there or not, but I'm sure they can't have been left out). Unfortunately there seem to be an oversight in the arrangements which left Brain standing at the bottom of the slope and everyone else standing at the top. Even with Brian conducting by waving his bow from side to side, his arm stretched up as high as he could, we couldn't see him. A dozen plus bases pounded away, but the various instruments and singing sections were all hopelessly out of time with each other, and we ground to a halt in a chaotic shambles.

"We can't see you," shouted the double bases to Brian.

"Take another step back," shouted some wag.

For a moment I thought the moment of "awesome fun" had arrived. Brian was standing on the edge of a six foot drop down onto the playing fields and I imagined him sailing backwards, still waving his bow, into the bushes below. Unfortunately Brian did not oblige and we launched into a second attempt of the song. I'm not sure it was any better than the first, but at least we reached the end and we could all go and take a break and wait with a sense of anticipation for the tutors end of course concert.

As a musician there is nothing quite like admiring the craft of those who are at the top of their game, demonstrating levels of skill that I can never imagine emulating. Amongst those who got up to dazzle us was John Paul on his mandolin.

"Hey," I nudged Jay, "that's the guy I told you about whose touring with Gillian Welsh and Dave Rawlings he's pretty good on that mandolin."

"Yes," agreed Jay, "that's John Paul Jones."

"Who's that?"

"The bass player from Led Zeppelin."

"Oh!"

It was a slightly weird thought that the bass player of the legendary rock group Led Zeppelin had been in my fiddling group all week and had been just a regular sort of guy, in fact really quiet and shy. There again why shouldn't he be, did I expect him to start head banging with his fiddle as he played *I'm on my Way Back to the Old Home,* although it might have been "awesome fun" if he had.

Jay and I arrived back from Sore Fingers with our friendship going through another difficult phase. Jay said he needed some time out, he thought we'd lost our connection which made it difficult for him to play music with me. We started to spend less time with each other; on top of that I no longer had the van for a musical retreat or to take us to any events. Although I had realised for some time that my sight problems meant I needed to get a smaller van to drive, I had figured I would have the transit until the conversion of the smaller one I had chosen was ready, but it wasn't to be.

Suddenly practicalities demanded it was sold and within two days it had gone because I was too feeble to state what I wanted. My friend Katie suggested I should go on assertive training course, an alarming idea, which I felt would probably need me to go on some sort of preliminary course to give me the courage to apply for such a thing. I was happy that the van was going to some local boys, who were going to use it as a gigging van, but my own needs were put on hold. What surprised me most was the lurch I felt every time I saw it driving around. I'd never felt an attachment to an inanimate object before, but I guess it was more than that for me. It was my escape pod and friend, and damn fine vehicle for transporting all the stuff that I had done over the last few years.

I have to admit that the car was a lot easier to drive, but useless when it came to stopping overnight, playing with your friend, or transporting a double bass to a gig to play some Country music for a Cowboy night at the local arts centre we had been asked to play at. Well, we'd have to do without the double bass, but Jimmi could play electric and we just had to choose a short list of songs to play after the film 'Butch Cassidy and the Sundance Kid' while the punters ate pork and beans. Didn't seem like a hard job, we'd get some money, hopefully enjoy ourselves and maybe sell a few books and CD's.

We arrived early at the venue to test the sound system. The film was still going on in the back room as Jimmy plugged in his Diplomat guitar to test it out. He let rip with bunch of notes and the alarmed manager rushed in with a loud "Shhhhhh", as *Raindrops Keep Falling on Your Head* was accompanied by more than just Paul Newman's smile. The rest of the sound check was a very hushed affair but the mics all seemed to work so we went to the bar for a drink.

One thing struck me as very strange, I wasn't nervous. I tried not to worry about this unusual state of affairs and continued to focus on feeling relaxed. It was going quite well until Jimmi turned to me with a slightly anxious look and said

"Are you nervous?"

"No," I assured him and once more turned away from any thoughts that might take me down that route.

"I always get a bit nervous," he confessed to me with a weak grin.

"I am not nervous," I said repeating my mantra and felt surprised that this was true. Perhaps the last few sessions we'd done at the local pub had steadied me, perhaps I just felt confident in what I was doing, or maybe I was suffering from some sort of psychosis?

Fortunately the last shoot out of Butch and Sundance took place, before I could conduct a full Freudian self-analysis, and we took our spots on the stage and struck up *Angeline the Baker*. We had played it Old Time, Bluegrass, Swing, and Rock a Billy styles, so why not Country? An immediate problem surfaced, the large hall had a horrible echo and, combined with the effects of the mics, the reverb bounced the notes all around the walls and up to the ceiling, before landing back in our ears. Without a feedback monitor the time delay made the sound effect similar to when you make a long distance call to Australia.

Things got worse as the punters sat down and started to talk and Jay started to sing. The colliding noises were horrible but we had to carry on grimly through the set before we could escape the cacophony. I had two numbers to sing, my first time singing with Outlaw Jones on stage, but there were no nerves, I was just appalled that this sound represented us. I don't know how it sounded to the audience, but nobody seemed to be paying much attention, they were head down in their beans or chatting to their neighbours. The end couldn't come soon enough.

I had left some CDs and books out on the front table but nobody took any notice or showed any signs they knew they were there. Maybe my lack of nerves was a premonition of what was about to come; as a shared musical experience it was a let-down and as a showcase of our musicianship a waste of time. A week later I sat in the garden at Dolwen discussing it with Jay, along with my inability to promote my book and CD. He looked at me sympathetically,

"Look, being a commercial success doesn't necessarily have anything to do with being good at something; it's about having the right contacts and promotion. People who value an honest acoustic sound enjoy what we do, but the music business is about business, not music."

"Guess so," I shrugged. I didn't have the desire, or energy, to spend my time promoting my music and writing, it was too boring and embarrassing. "Anyway, let's play some stuff to the flowers."

The flowers at Dolwen were a great audience, very beautiful, completely wild, appreciatively quiet, and danced gently in the soft breeze to our music. My own satisfaction with the book and CD should be enough, and if other people happened across them and enjoyed them, then it was a bonus. Most people that had read my book appeared to have enjoyed it, although I wasn't sure if the concept, about the way the music and book related to each other, was fully understood. This hadn't been helped by technical difficulties of getting the music to play on mobile devices used for eBooks, problems which I had been unaware of when creating the links.

The links were fine when using a normal computer, but to work on mobile devices they needed a flash player to be embedded in our website. This information had finally been extracted from the Kindle, after weeks of calls and emails, to lands far, far away. The solution was expensive and in the end Jay uploaded the tracks on SoundCloud, a free audio website that allows you to share your music. I changed the links to match and my project was finally finished.

...

It seemed like the end of an era, not only was my book and CD completed, but Crazy had gone. Her and Seb finally seemed to be sorted after hitting their darkest hour, first it was all off, and then it was all back on again. It was an emotionally draining time, and that was just from my point of view, but Crazy weathered the storm and stayed true to her belief that her and Seb were meant to be together. Seb finally realised this too, and within a few weeks of it dawning on him, Jules had moved in with him. At last she had found her 'happily ever after' and was with someone as crazy as she was. I have to admit I missed her at first, she was the ideal flat mate, I didn't see a lot of her but when she was around she was a good friend and we'd shared lots of laughs and run lots of miles together, but I soon got used to living alone.

Fortunately, I enjoyed my own company, but it was nice to share some things, music being one of them, so I was glad that after a period of reflection Jay had done some soul searching and was now easier company to be around. We wrote a few tunes and did some recording; I often made up tunes, but then couldn't remember them, so hearing them back was useful. As Jay and I were now getting on better I started to wonder whether we could go to the Conwy Bluegrass festival together and if the new van would be ready to take us. We been for the last four years and usually looked forward to it, however having had the luxury of a van for my last three visits I was reluctant to go without one. I harried the dealer to finish the conversion and two days before the festival started it was ready. I caught a train to

Worcester and a bus to the garage and arrived in the afternoon, slightly nervous as it would be the first time I'd be seeing the van I was buying.

When I arrived Phil was still screwing the number plates on, and once he finished we went into the office. He handed me the paper work with a bright smile, "Right all ready to go. We just need to have a quick chat about some of the important things that you should be aware of, the main one being the water coolant alarm. If that comes on you need to stop immediately, well as soon as you can do safely, and then call me so we can recommend a garage in the area that can deal with it. Don't let anybody else touch it, they may say they know what to do but don't believe them, it's very easy to wreck the engine unless it's fixed correctly."

Phil reiterated the same instructions several times until he seemed absolutely sure that I understood the importance of what he was saying and the catastrophic consequences for the engine should it fall into the wrong hands. By the time he finished I was convinced the van was a ticking time bomb with the water coolant waiting to go off as soon as I had driven around the corner. I can't remember anything else he said after his dire warnings; his voice went on in the background as I wondered when the calamity would strike.

"Ok, so here you go," he said cheerily handing me the keys.

I took them cautiously and went out to the van and got into the driver's seat.

"Put them in here," Phil said standing by the open driver's door and pointing to the ignition.

Bravely I stuck them in and looked for the gear stick. It was then I noticed it was an automatic. When I tried out similar vehicles I had only been concerned with the width of the van rather than how it was driven. I felt a bit stupid.

"Err I haven't driven an automatic before," I admitted.

"Oh it's easy, most people prefer them, you'll be fine. You just need the D for drive, R for reverse and P is for park. Don't worry about anything else."

"But what are they for?" I said starring at the other letters on the control stick.

"Oh nothing important," he said dismissing the other four other potential positions for the lever.

"What's this for?" I said stabbing my left foot at a little wedge in the foot-well.

"It's just to rest your foot on."

"And this?" I said poking a strange box below the radio.

"I'm not sure, maybe a DVD player?"

"Does the radio work?"

"I don't know, anyway don't worry about that, why don't you turn the engine on?"

Phil seemed to operate on a need to know basis, and it appeared most things I didn't need to know. Carefully I turned the ignition and waited for something to explode. There was a beep, red lights went on and off on the dash board, except one, and a lady said something to me in Japanese.

"What's that?" I said suspiciously looking at the red light.

"Err, you need petrol. Try putting it drive."

"Where's the nearest petrol station, have I got enough to get there?"

"Yes, you'll be fine; it's just down the road."

"And the Japanese lady?"

"Oh don't worry about her."

I decided that the mysterious Japanese lady was the least of my problems and put the lever into drive while looking for my clutch. I rolled forward a few yards, stopped, and put it into park.

"There you go, sorted!" Phil's head appeared through the window and it appeared my lesson was over. I attached Seb's trusty Sat Nav to the dashboard and Tim's reassuring voice came on, unperturbed by the constant interruptions from the Japanese lady he guided me home. Later I discovered that her voice belonged to a Japanese Sat Nav system and I guess she was saying something like "Turn left to Okinawa." I had her removed, she would never be happy that far from home and I didn't think Tim approved of her either.

It was two days till Conway and despite the rush to get the van ready for the festival I suddenly didn't feel that inspired about going. The forecast for the first two days was heavy rain and I'd seen all the bands play before and wasn't bothered about seeing them again. It might have been fun to hook up with the Muddy River Boys, the band that Jay used to play with, but that didn't seem like a good enough reason for the cost of going. Bob, the bass player from the Muddies, had phoned Jay not long after we'd released our CD. He had said he was never going to speak to Jay again, after Jay had accidently sent him a less than complimentary text, but he appeared to have recovered from this unfortunate event. I was at Dolwen when he rang.

"What did he say?" I asked Jay afterwards.

"He's heard our CD. Guess what he thought?" he said with a grin.

"It was 'Faantastic?"

"Yep, he hasn't changed."

"Faantastic" was Bob's favourite catch phrase and I'm glad he liked the music. It would have been fun to play with him again, but with Jay equally as disinterested about attending this year's Conwy festival as me, we decided not to go. Nonetheless I still wanted to try the van out.

"Shall I come over to yours on Saturday and we'll just go somewhere for the evening, have a play and test things out?" I suggested to Jay.

"Okay sounds like fun, see you then."

Saturday was sunny and fine and we chucked our bedding and instruments in the back and headed off. I was hungry and we didn't get very far down the road before we stopped in the car park next to the Prince Harry pub, and had something to eat. A few years before we use to play regularly in the Prince Harry with the Muddy River Boys. I had been banned for being too 'Jazzy' so we didn't go there anymore, but sometimes stopped to play in the adjacent car-park. This had beautiful views across the estuary and once we had finished our lunch we got the instruments out. The afternoon past pleasantly, people had stopped to listen and clap, another car-park user had brought us over some beer, and nobody said I was playing the wrong kind of music.

The hills that rose above the water, on the far side of the estuary, basked in the warm sunshine and when Jay said there was a panoramic walk way, along the top that he had walked years before, we went to find it. He remembered where the turning was to take the steep road which led to the top and drove the Bongo up the precipitous hairpin bends, only making me scream a few times. I may have lost a lot of space by downsizing to the Bongo but the Transit would have never made it up the track. The views looking down on the estuary were stunning and we could think of no better place to spend the night than back at the car-park we had just left. With a pop up roof I slept 'upstairs' and Jay slept 'downstairs', it was surprisingly peaceful and I slept quite well. It was a relief to spend time with Jay and feel relaxed and untroubled by his emotions for me, maybe we had both moved on and we could put the past behind us.

Chapter 4. Old Haunts

There is something about a closet that makes a skeleton terribly restless. (Wilson Mizner)

Of course putting the past behind you can be a difficult thing, you can try and disconnect from it for a while but it catches up with you in all kinds of ways, especially when matters are left unresolved, as in the case of Jay and Jimmi's former home, Shady Grove. Since Jimmi had left the housing Co-operative, neither he nor Jay had been back there. Jimmi was so angry that he had just walked away, leaving virtually all his possessions behind. He felt the bad blood between himself and Madge and Mysterious Jack had poisoned all that he cherished about Shady Grove and resulted in the torrid time that he and Jay had endured at the camp under the rule of the Corleone brothers. Now circumstances had changed and a new family had moved into the cottage he and Jay used to share, and we heard that Kate, who lived in the small house next door with her husband, Sam, had terminal cancer. After a short battle she passed away.

I felt so sorry for Sam, he and Kate had always seemed such a complete couple it was difficult to imagine him without her. I remembered the last time I had seen Kate when I had been running on the seafront and had noticed a lady starring wistfully out to sea. With my poor eyesight I had already gone passed her by the time I realised it was Kate. I carried on running and debating in my mind what I should do. Should I run back and disturb her moment of reflection and if I did what would I say? What could I say? I decided to leave her in peace, but felt I had taken the cowardly option.

I didn't go to the funeral. Kate was being buried in grounds of Shady Grove and I didn't feel close enough to Sam to feel comfortable about going to a family affair. Jimmi and Jay decided to put their differences with Co-Op behind them, especially knowing that their old adversaries from the Co-Op, Madge and Jack weren't going to be there, and they went to say goodbye to Kate and console Sam. Inadvertently they found that the day helped to heal their own wounds and introduced them to the new family now living at Shady Grove; Ally, Steve and their children.

Both Jimmi and Jay started visiting The Grove again, liking the new people who had moved in and re-kindling their relationship with Sam. Jimmi retrieved some of his possessions, which had been stacked in his poly tunnel since his departure, bringing them back to Dolwen. It added to the clutter which had gradually amassed since he and Jay had moved in, making the improvements of the recent refurbishment increasingly difficult to see. The house was not looking at its best for prospective buyers, but Jay had put it on the market, keen to release himself from the burden of the mortgage he had acquired. As ever he was optimistic things would turn out well, and that there might even be enough money left, after he had sold it, for him and Jimmi to buy a share in their own Co-operative.

For the moment Jimmi appeared to be happy in his new home, there was plenty of room for friends to stay, and the lounge had now become a studio where he could produce records. There was also good internet access so he could spend hours of uninterrupted time chatting on Facebook; bringing to light the various conspiracies weaved by the corporations, banks and politicians. Over winter, of the two different places Jimmi slept in the house, his bedroom and the couch in the sitting room, the latter had been his preferred place to wage his war on the establishment. It was warm, next door to the kitchen and had the best internet connection, so he could listen to the presenter Alex Jones, ranting on about the political scum bags in the White House. Most people like something soothing to send them to sleep, but for Jimmi an angry, shouty man was his preferred lullaby.

As the weather became warmer Jimmi decided that he liked sleeping closer to the sky and cleared out a spot in the attic to make a den up in the roof space. He also ventured up the steep garden to sit and bask in the sun, warming up his Mediterranean blood, and pick the herbs and berries in the garden which had been left to run wild. There were raspberries, strawberries, Saint John's Wort, Comfrey, Sage, in fact a whole medicine cabinet waiting to be harvested by those who knew what they were gathering. Jimmi loved to cook and scattered the ingredients from the garden on the food he made. Jay was in charge of the cleaning, and although there was occasional bickering and frictions between the two of them, for the first six months they muddled along, putting up with each other's idiosyncrasies.

Dolwen wasn't as convenient as the camp had been for me to meet up and play with Jay, but once I had the new van our musical rendezvous became more mobile. By early summer the weather was gorgeous and it was great to pop the roof up, put the kettle on the little stove, and play sitting outside. One day we were playing on the seafront, when a familiar figure came striding into view with a dog trotting alongside. It was Security Larry, the camp guard from where Jay and Jimmi lived the previous summer. Occasionally I caught sight of Larry out of the corner of my eye as I drove through the town but hadn't actually talked to him since the guys had left the camp last September. He hadn't changed; he was wearing his battered straw hat and carrying a small lumpy brown sack. It was lovely to see him and I gave him a hug.

"Ah can't stop," Ah'm off t'bowls," he said in his slow Lancashire accent, waving the sack as evidence of his mission. "Ah'm going t' be late but come an' see me soon." We waved him goodbye and reminisced a bit about the camp while I put the tea on. The period when the guys had been living at the camp had been a strange time, but meeting Larry there had been one of the good things that had happened. Our brief encounter with him prompted me to called by at the camp a couple of days later, taking him a gift of a book and CD, knowing how much he enjoyed our music and liked to read.

As I pushed back the security gate it was like going back in time, and looking around at the old barrack buildings I half expected to see the creepy Bruno or his twin brother Carlo, who had nominally run the camp for a while, pop out of the gatehouse. Fortunately they were long gone but I was glad to drive around the corner away from the unpleasant memories of being banned by them from visiting Jay and Jimmi in the accommodation block. I parked in front of the big old rusty wagon, where Larry lived, and shouted a greeting as I approached the truck. The pirates and the ship on the dash board looked back silently through the front screen, but Bob Dog heard and came out to greet me. This meant Larry couldn't be far away, and I walked round the back of the stationary vehicle whose large, black wheels were embedded firmly in the tall grass.

The old piles of tyres that Larry had been using as a make shift pen for his donkeys were now being used as planters for potatoes and tomatoes, and it looked like his garden was doing well. I wondered where the donkeys were and shouted again and knocked on the side of the truck. A muffled response came from inside and I poked my head through the open door to see a rather dishevelled Larry rubbing his face and I caught the waft of alcohol from the dim interior.

"Hello, Jess, lovely to see yer, come on in," Larry looked a bit befuddled.

"How you doing?" I asked him. "Thought I'd pop by, I've got something for you."

"Have you?" Larry perked up.

"Yes I'll just get it from the van," I said and ducked out the door taking a deep breath. Glyn, another camp resident, was approaching with a bunch of wires and some tools.

"Hi, Larry, I just need to see if I can fix this up, I think you've got a connection that'll work," he ducked inside the truck despite Larry's uncertain look. By the time I returned Glyn was fiddling in the roof behind the drivers' seat, yanking some wiring down.

"For you," I said to Larry, passing him the book and CD around the side of Glyn's legs, "they go together."

A big smile lit up Larry's face and he held my gifts carefully like precious china, admiring them, "You couldn't give me anything better than a book and music." The delight was written all over his face and I bashfully tried to play down my present. "No, Ah mean it, Ah'm dead chuffed," he said, dismissing my embarrassment, "what more could you possibly give me than something to read and something to listen to?" I couldn't think of an answer but his appreciation made me feel really warm inside, and I felt he had given me a gift equally as special.

He sat down to examine them more closely, "Come on in," he said encouragingly as I hovered in the doorway, "have a seat," he said pointing to the couch that ran along one wall. I sat down cautiously in my white trousers, mesmerised by the long brown belt hanging from the roof. This revealed itself, when my eyes were fully adjusted to the dark interior, as a sticky fly catcher with at least a hundred flies stuck to it.

"Careful!" he said and I jumped up again looking carefully at the seat cover. I was sure I'd sat on the cleanest bit.

"If you lean yer head back there you'll staple it t' wall," he said, pointing to row of sharp screws sticking out of a piece of wood, waiting to impale unwary heads to them.

"Oh thanks," I said heeding his advice and moving down to the less dangerous end of the couch. Larry turned his attention back to the book and CD.

"Look at the lovely picture," he said admiring the CD cover.

"It's taken just above Dolwen and the picture on the book cover is my fiddle, Jay's hat and Jimmi's scarf." I said showing him. "It's all about my musical adventures and you're in the second part when the guys move to the camp."

"Best times Ah've had since Ah've been here," he said wistfully.

"Yeah, happy days apart from crazy Carlo and Bruno," I qualified his comment. "Anyway, what's happen to your donkeys?"

Larry's face clouded over, "Ah was told Ah had to get rid of them, because of all the complaints, an' they were so happy running around free here."

I remembered it hadn't taken much for Lenny and Dennis to act like their wild ancestors and leave their pen to seek the wide open spaces of the camp, ensuring an ongoing battle of wits between them and their sometime keeper, Larry.

"But they're okay aren't they?"

"Yes, but they've been institutionalised in a donkey sanctuary, and would have been much happier here. Anyway, Ah'm not stopping here much longer, once they've had the vote and powers been decentralised I'm off to Scotland. Ah'll be gone in September."

"Where you going to stay?"

"In ma van."

"When did you last take it out on the road?"

"Four years ago. It'll pass MOT tomorrow," he added proudly.

I thought of the rusty holes in the exterior bodywork and the grass growing over the wheels and wondered how he could be so sure.

"It's just the cost of the insurance, Ah had a quote for over eight hundred pounds, that's what put me back on the drink," he said apologetically. "Ah been off it fer a month, but that tipped me over the edge, though it doesn't take much," he said shaking his head. "Anyway I reckon it's the place to be, there's nothing for me here. Scotland's best place in the world fer New Year goes on fer a fortnight and yer get a free drink at any house you call at."

Glyn laughed from his position behind the of spaghetti wires, "Yeah that'll be heaven for you all right."

Larry smiled, "Can yer lend me a tenner," he asked Glyn hopefully, "I need baccy and alcohol."

"Well what about a fiver and choose between baccy and alcohol," said Glyn, holding out one fiver of the two he'd found in his pocket. I wondered if Glyn was running his own self-help support group and this was his way of helping Larry cut back on the toxic substances that ruled his life.

"Ah need both," said Larry firmly. "If Ah could just do this job, Ah know about, then Ah'd have enough money to get me to Scotland," he looked at me furtively. "They just need to be unconscious fer fifteen minutes, well twenty; one of those Taser guns should do it. It's illegal of course," he said apologetically.

I looked at him and frowned. Larry and a potential heist did not sound a good combination, I could only think it would end in disaster for everyone concerned, especially Larry, and I wasn't going to encourage him by condoning his plan.

"Well nobody's gone t' get hurt and he shouldn't have the money in the first place," he said indignantly.

I wasn't sure whether Larry was trying to convince me or himself of the righteousness of his actions.

"Larry I really don't think you should tell me anymore," I said hurriedly before he could divulge any more damming revelations, "anyway, I need to go; I'm meeting Jay at Shady Grove. I'll come and see you soon, enjoy the book."

"Thanks Jess, Ah'll come and do the gate."

As we got into my van, Glyn seemed to be trying to attach an aerial to the bonnet of Larry's vehicle.

"Is Glyn fixing a CB radio to your truck?" I asked Larry

"Ah bloody hope not," said Larry, "last thing I want to do is talk to anybody. All that 'do you copy,' rubbish," he shook his head in disgust and I left the camp none the wiser what either Glyn or Larry were up to.

I drove on to Shady Grove; I was meeting Jay and Jimmi up there for a curry with Ally and Steve. I parked up by what used to be the old boiler house but had now been turned into a smart wooden outhouse. There'd been some changes since the new people had moved in. I got out and was hailed from the direction of Sam's house, Jimmi and Jay had already arrived and were having a drink with him. I walked in and there was Sam, all smiley and lovely. We shared a big hug, it was great to be back, and while we all chatted, Sam put on a huge pot of rice to share with the curry being cooked by Ally next door.

When it was ready we took it round to the cottage, which had also had a bit of a make-over since Jay and Jimmi lived there, looking much better for it. The present family seemed like the right people for the space; Steve was a spiritualist and Ally liked to grow things and sing. Her voice went really well with Jay's and they had started to work on some songs together. I wished I could do the same. Jay said I just had to let go, but I didn't believe him. I didn't feel my voice had the basic qualities to be a good singer, joining in with a bit of a sing along was about as far as it went and after we had eaten Ally's delicious curry we all got some instruments out and sang and played the evening away.

It wasn't long before I returned to Shady Grove, but this time my mission was different, I'd come back to see Steve and try 'regression therapy', both Jay and Jimmi had had a session with him and I was curious to experience it for myself. Evidently he had put them in a light hypnosis and then led them back into previous lives to learn more about themselves. I'd never done anything like it before and asked Steve if I could try it.

He took me upstairs to the small room which used to belong to "Mysterious Jack". There were lots of coloured crystals on the window shelf and a mattress on the floor with pillows and a blanket. I made myself comfortable on the mattress while Steve closed the window and drew the blind and put on some gentle music. It was a warm day and I felt very relaxed and with Steve talking softly in the background and soon wanted to go to sleep, which I probably would have done if Steve hadn't kept asking me questions. I was so drowsy I found it difficult to stir myself to say anything.

I tried harder to walk through the door that Steve had suggested I open see a past life. I decided I was somewhere hot and dry, a desert like place, maybe somewhere in the Middle East, and I was a man with dark skin, a beard and a long white cotton thawb. I was standing alone on a dirt road with no other sign of habitation, I wasn't sure what I was doing there, how I got there, or where I was going, but Steve was persistent in his efforts to find out. Eventually I thought my last known contact with other people was at a coffee house and could see myself standing on the edge of a crowd of men, all wearing thawbs, who were arguing about something. In the middle of the group was a man counting shekels, he looked strangely like Jimmi doing a Sheik of Araby impression and the argument appeared to be about money.

I couldn't see anything else about this previous existence; I seemed to have no family or friends but was quite comfortable being alone rather than part of the aggressive atmosphere I had witnessed in the coffee house. Steve then took me to my last day in that life, where I was lying on a bed on the floor being given a drink of water by an old woman, I don't know who she was but she seemed quite nice. I was tired and died quite peacefully of old age. Steve asked me about the after-life, which felt pleasant, if a little hazy, and was bit like being a bright floating spirit bubble, rising up with other spirit bubbles floating by.

When it was over I'm not sure what I thought about it all really. Poor Steve had beads of sweat running down his face, the room was sweltering. I wondered whether my visions were 'real' thoughts or was I just trying to please Steve and respond to his questions. Whatever the 'reality' of my experience was it had all been very relaxing and made me realise that essentially I liked being alone without people hassling me, wherever I was.

...

I began to be drawn back into more individual pursuits and returned to sailing after a three year absence. It was good to be out on the water again, just me, the boat, and the elements. I decided to race again; I was a bit concerned about awakening the competitive side of me, which I wasn't sure produced particularly productive emotions. To my surprise, and relief, it didn't happen. I enjoyed getting the boat to perform to the best of my ability and I even enjoyed seeing youngsters, who started sailing a few years back, going past me. The physical challenge was satisfying but it was also time to seek out some new mental stimulation and try a different instrument. I thought I knew what that would be.

I had been attracted to the cello for some time and had already purchased a five string violin which has the same strings as a cello, except for the top E. The cello was originally popularised by the change in vocal trends in Western Europe in the Middle Ages, from a high nasal pitch to a lower sound, making it a common accompanying instrument for the bass line in musical pieces. Gradually its stunning resonance had become more widely recognised, and its potential as a solo instrument was brought to prominence by J.S Bach's six suites for the cello. As a standard part of a string quartet and a symphony orchestra, many sonatas and concertos have been written for the cello by Haydn, Beethoven, Brahms and Elgar to mention a few eminent composers. Outside classical music it is also used for the Blues, Folk, Bluegrass, and Jazz which was where my interest lay.

I scoured the internet for deals and in the end decided to go for a low risk, quality student instrument from the German makers, Stentor, I ordered it and sat and waited...and waited. I think I must have fallen asleep and was dreaming I was at Dolwen, sitting at the table with Jay, talking to Bumbalina, who hovered above it on her magic carpet on a flying visit from another world. I knew it was Bumbalina because I never really understood what she was saying. She was very spiritual and spent a lot of time meditating and dealing with inner conflicts, which was very exhausting for her and required a special diet, which was why she wasn't eating pizza with us. She and Jay conversed in the same language of "energy fields, narcissistic projections and vibrational attractions", and I listened to their curious meanderings as I finished my tea.

Jimmi walked in carrying a tool box and a strange plastic object which looked like a giant pair of soldering goggles. I did a double take and replayed the scene slowly. Had I seen correctly? Not only that, but Bumbalina got off her magic carpet to make him a meal like a dutiful house wife. Obviously I was in one of Steve's regression sessions living some past life.

"What's that Jimmi," I said picking up the strange giant googles.

"It's for the car, I made it specially to blank out the air bag failure warning light so the car will pass its MOT, otherwise I'll have to pay £600 for a new airbag."

"How's it going to work?" I asked curiously.

"Come and see." Jimmi seemed quite excited by his invention and we went out to his car and I got into the passenger seat while Jimmi sat in the driver's side. The casing of the dashboard and steering column had been taken out and Jimmi poked the dials through the holes of the giant googles which now revealed themselves as a new dashboard casing, with a thicker band going across the offending light and effectively blanking it out. Jimmi carefully slotted it back into the dashboard and clipped the casing around the wires in the steering column.

"Perfect," Jimmi smiled and then frowned. The speedo metre was fixed at 60 mph and we were stationary. Jimmi yanked it all out again and repeated the whole process with the dial corrected to zero this time. We went back inside where Bumbalina was cooking tofu and garlic and fussing around the kitchen.

"How was your day at work?" she asked Jimmi.

"I really enjoyed it," he said enthusiastically. I closed my eyes and the smell of garlic wafted gently up my nose like powerful incense. I was definitely dreaming.

When I awoke I was on Facebook. I had only joined in the last few weeks, and found it a strange 'reality'; however it was often the best means of getting in touch with some people. It was also an easy way of being less isolated, without the discomfort of actually socialising. I could look briefly in on what other people were doing, catch up with friends I hadn't seen for years, and do several other things all at the same time. It did require some slightly different language and social skills which I was picking up as I went along. You had a thing called a timeline which you could put things on, which I did occasionally, but usually I just scanned what other people were posting.

One evening I noticed a lady in the village had posted she was feeling sad and several people had sent a response, extending their sympathy and support. She always seemed such a positive lady I thought she must be feeling very low to write such a thing. Eventually I worked out how to put some cheering music on her timeline, and then the insanity of what I'd done struck me. If I got on my bike it would probably only take me a minute to ride down the road and see her, so I did. As it turned out she was away, but it made me think what a curious world we lived, where we could be so close to people, but so far away.

I carried on in my own state of splendid state of isolation. My cello had finally arrived, with a phone call from the delivery man.

"Jesse Jones? I have a package for you, a violin I think?"

"I hope not," I presumed the man's musical knowledge was a little wanting as the package I was expecting should be about ten times larger than a violin.

"Oh well can you can come and meet me as I can't get under the bridge."

"Ok, I'll be there in a few minutes."

I threw a coat on and raced down to meet him. Fortunately the package was the size I was expecting and carefully I took it back home and unwrapped the large box. There it was, my new cello looking all shiny and grand. I sat down and pulled out the end piece and stood it between my legs with the long neck placed over my left shoulder. I put a tuner on the bridge and plucked a string. Not surprisingly it was out of tune and the tuning pegs were large and stiff and took both my hands to adjust. Twenty minutes later I'd finally done it and picked up the bow and tightened it, before drawing it across the C string. A deep growly note came out and I changed the angle and then played the G, D, and A strings in turn, the resonance of the sound made the air around me rumble.

Although the cello is very different to the violin, the basic principles of drawing a sound out with a bow and using a finger board without frets were the same. I found I could draw a good sound out on the open strings straight away but making a fretted note was a lot harder. I needed help and found a series of online lessons with a kind European man, possibly Germanic, who I decided to call Gunter.

Gunter dressed himself very particularly in a crisp white shirt with a bow tie. His instructions were very clear and precise, although I had a feeling that without any musical knowledge they would be a bit difficult to follow.

"Dear friends, this is our beloved cello," Gunter began solemnly, remarking on the instrument held between his knees, and I was off on the great cello adventure. It wasn't that I still didn't have a lot more to master on the violin; I just wanted the rush of a new challenge and the thrill of those first giant steps of learning a new instrument. I hadn't told Jay and Jimmi about getting a cello, I thought I'd wait till I felt a little more competent on it, but wasn't sure how long that would take.

I was still spending time practicing the violin every day, we had a bank holiday session coming up in a local pub, and a few days later were playing at the County show. I went over to Dolwen on the Saturday night for the pub session, and we sat waiting for Ally to turn up. She'd been doing some practise with Jay and Jimmi but hadn't performed for some years and was a little anxious about it. She phoned before she left, and Jimmi reassured her that there was nothing to worry about, it was just a low key event. I was surprised; she seemed a very confident person, although you never knew what people felt inside.

Eventually she arrived and was chatty and nervous, "Just need a drink before we go," she said hurriedly and pulled out a bottle of wine, like a magician, and rolled a cigarette. We all sat watching her.

"I'll see you there," I said as the tension started to get to me and I left in my own vehicle.

When I arrived the pub was warm and bright and quite busy. Matt was already there, relaxed after a holiday with his family, and when the others joined us we settled down with our drinks, tuned up, and Matt started to sing. He had a loud and confident voice, which was just as well as the sound got absorbed by the surrounding furniture and people. Jimmi was the only one with an amp and the rest of us had to work really hard to raise the volume above the general background noise. Ally had a whole pile of songs with her and I was surprised how much she and Jay had covered in the short period of time they'd been practising. I joined in with bits on the fiddle where I could and was quite glad to take it easy, casually leaning against a pillar. More people came into the bar.

"Ma names Stewie, what's yours?" A Scottish voice intruded on my somnolence.

"Jesse."

"Well Jesse, ken yer play more fiddle? I love the fiddle and you ken play, com'on give us a tune."

I was slightly flattered by his drunken admiration and also taken back by being spotted from my position of safety behind the pillar. Ally and Matt had gone to get more drinks so it was hard to find an excuse not to oblige. I launched into *Gypsy Sway* with the help of Jay and Jimmi; Stewie smiled happily and bought me a drink. I thanked him and went back to my repose behind the pillar.

"Hi, ma names Douggie, ken you play more fiddle?" another Scottish voice nagged me. I wondered whether there was some problem in the space, time continuum, which had resulted in me being in Scotland on Burns night, it sure didn't seem like an August Bank holiday in Wales. I gave a nod to Jay and we began our Irish medley, which started slowly with the *Boat Song*, before launching into a full on reel with *Buskers Fantasy* and *Morrison's Reel.* Ally gave a scream and leapt to her feet clapping her hands above her head and jumping up and down. The Scottish contingent in the pub needed no encouragement and joined in the manoeuvre, going into a pogo dancing frenzy, perhaps the equivalent of a reel in the land north of Hadrian's Wall.

The wild shrieks and thumps meant nobody could hear the music and they were all dancing out of time, but it didn't put them off. Stewie pirouetted by, looking like the Irish dancer, Michele Flattery, on speed, and as I watched the chaotic scene in-front of me, I harked back to an early ambition, of wanting to inspire people to dance. Well, I could tick that one off, but if I didn't stop soon we would probably be calling for an ambulance due to the over ambitious athletics taking place in the tight space.

There was a sigh of disappointment as the tune ended, but I think Dawn, the pub landlady, was pleased as there were clients in residence upstairs and she suggested we might like to play on in the pool room. We moved next door. Douggie was hassling me to play more.

"Ah just want to hear the fiddle, just the fiddle. You play a piece by yourself," he told me and the crowd that had followed us into the pool room. Anything for a quiet life, I played my tune Solstice that I had written, on the named day, earlier in the summer. I seemed to have lost the nerves that had paralysed my public playing, but I was struggling to convey the passion that I felt, maybe it was just too personal.

"Ock that was lovely but yer play within yourself," Douggie observed, "you've got to give it out more to the audience."

Douggie might have imbibed a fair amount of alcohol, but his observation was correct. His friend Archie was also trying to tell me something, but Matt and the crowd had launched into *The Sloop John B* and it was difficult to communicate and overcome the noise of the raucous singing. I would have to get closer to hear what Archie was saying, but this looked potentially dangerous, he was very drunk; I decided it was time to leave and let the party continue without me.

A few days later I was driving up to Bala to meet Jay at the County Show and take part in the musical entertainment. I was going to do a folk set with him, and Jimmi and Ally were joining us later, Ally was going do a set with Jay and Jimmi and then they would do an Outlaw Jones set with me. There was also going to be another couple playing, Ken and Odessa, who had already played a set by the time I had arrived and we were letting us use their sound system. The tent we were playing in was next to the beer tent, where people were casually standing and sitting around as we provided some background entertainment to their drinking.

There was no pressure, my fiddle was sounding quite nice through the PA, and I felt relaxed as I skipped through our folk tunes. By the time we had finished Jimmi and Ally had arrived and quickly sorted out their gear and did their songs. Once they had finished I went round the back of tent, to where the car was parked, to get some money and buy them all a drink, I also took my fiddle. When Jay and I had sorted out the Outlaw Jones set, the previous day, there had been a couple of songs I hadn't played for a while and I thought I better quickly reassure myself I could still remember them. Five minutes later I was happy and put by fiddle down in the car boot, picked up my purse and shut the boot.

I turned back to car with a slight feeling of concern, I couldn't remember where I'd put the car keys. I checked my pockets, nothing; I starred at the car boot suspiciously and tried to lift it. It was locked. I sped round to the front of the car and tried the doors but they were all locked. The horror dawned on me, not only were the car keys locked inside the boot, but also my fiddle. I could hear that Ken and Odessa had started their second set; I had about forty five minutes to sort it out before I was due on with Outlaw Jones.

I quickly informed Jay and Jimmi of the situation and they both tried all the doors and agreed with me they were locked and we all stared at the vehicle helplessly. My next thought was to run to the bar and seek help, barman always knew about these things didn't they? Maybe if I could find someone with the same car their keys would open mine? The barman shook his head

"That won't work, but I did see this thing on Top Gear once. You got a spare set of keys somewhere?"

"Yes, back at the house."

"Well they got someone to click the spare keys down the phone to their mobile and then held it against the car door and that unlocked it."

I stared at him amazed by his incredible suggestion, but I was desperate.

"Okay, thanks."

I went back to the car got my mobile out my pocket and started to phone everyone I knew back in my home village. The children were out but the house wasn't locked and if I could find someone to help they walk in, pick up the spare keys and save the day, however nobody was answering. I kept trying and finally Sue (of Harriet the Hamster fame) picked up.

"Sue I'm having a crisis, blah, blah, blah, locked keys and fiddle in boot, blah, blah, blah, use spare keys and mobile phone, blah, blah, blah…"

To my amazement Sue seemed to grasp what I was on about and agreed to nip round to the house and be the technical operator in my dubious plan. Ten minutes later I called her, she was at the house, found the spare keys and part one of the operation was complete.

"Right hold them against the phone, where you normally speak, keep pressing the unlock button and pray."

I ran back over to the car, as in order to hear what Sue was saying I had to be a short distance away from the music tent and the sound of Ken and Odessa playing. I got on my knees by the car door and pressed the phone against the lock and offered up my own prayers. Nothing happened. I ran back to the communication zone.

"What about trying Ben's phone?" (I could hear her son Ben running around in the background as a member of the support staff). "Okay great, give me two seconds."

I ran back to the car and held my mobile against the lock…nothing happened. I pressed my head against the lock and pointed my phone at it though my head. I heard somewhere that brain waves are good conductors of car key signals. I prayed harder and could feel Sue and Ben were doing the same down the other end of the phone, although I doubted if they were on their knees like me…nothing happened. I ran back to the communication zone.

"Try the house phone."

I ran back to the car and went into my position of supplication...nothing happened. I ran back to the communication zone.

"Try the upstairs phone."

I ran back to the car and screwed up my eyes with concentration...but nothing happened. Slowly I went back to the communication zone, I was nearly beaten.

"Sue I don't suppose you'd meet me half way at Cross Foxes with the keys? The PA system is going at six, so we'd still have enough time to play our set, if you could... Brilliant, thanks so much."

I went to ask Jimmi if he could drive me there and we set off, managing to arrive a couple of minutes before Sue did. The worrying thought I'd had, that Sue might have brought the wrong set of keys with her, was unfounded and in less than an hour we were back in Bala. I dashed to the car, grabbed my fiddle, and went straight on stage with the guys and played our set. I still had the adrenaline of the key drama coursing around my body but was elated that with a little help from my friends the hurdles had been overcome and I still had a chance to play. We ripped through our swing numbers and I found myself playing in the breaks of *Sweet Georgia Brown,* in places that I hadn't visited before. Jay said he'd never heard me play so well in front of an audience, but I hoped I wouldn't have to repeat the afternoon's saga to play with the same abandonment again.

I came off stage all smiles and sat down with Ken and Odessa who had heroically held the fort and played on and on until I had returned from my mission. Ally wanted to do one more set with Jay and Jimmi before Ken and Odessa had to leave taking the PA system with them. I could see that Jimmi had had enough, and was a reluctant participant in proceedings. There was going to be trouble.

Jimmi considered himself a professional musician and felt he should be paid. We were only getting expenses and it made him feel like he was getting ripped off, after all, as he often said, you wouldn't expect an electrician or plumber to do a job for you for free, so why should he as a musician of some forty years' experience. I could sympathise with what he was saying, people were always turning up at Dolwen and asking him to do recordings for free. When he helped to the CD for Outlaw Jones I had paid him, but it would have been a lot more if I had gone to a professional studio.

Jimmi did a few songs with Jay and Ally before he decided that the set had finished and put his guitar down. He was persuaded to do a couple more, which he did with ill grace, before walking off angrily to go and have a smoke in the car. I helped pack the gear up. Ally was upset and Jay was cross, and he departed once we had sorted the gear. I got Jimmi and Ally a drink and they both calmed down and the dust apparently settled. However, that afternoon had awakened old ghosts that hung around the fringes of the three of us in Outlaw Jones, starting a chain of events that none of us could have foreseen.

Chapter 5. Parting of the Ways

Don't cry because it's over, smile because it happened.
(Dr Seuss)

Jimmi took Ally back to Shady Grove and spent the night there. Since Kate's funeral he'd been visiting quite a lot and become friendly with Ally and her family. He was hopeful that Madge and Jack would leave the community, and if they did, he might be able to go back and live in their cottage, engaging in the lifestyle he had originally envisaged when he moved to the area. The resentments that he felt surrounding his departure from Shady Grove gnawed away at him. When he had woken up the next day his grievances had spilled out, with Ally on the receiving end. There was little she could do to change the past and he arrived back at Dolwen upset, facing the possibility that he might not go back to live at Shady Grove again.

It didn't help that he and Jay were no longer comfortable housemates, the 'for sale' sign a constant reminder to Jimmi that his base at Dolwen was only temporary. On top of that there were their musical differences. Later that day they had 'words' and Jay texted me that Jimmi no longer wanted to play with Outlaw Jones. This didn't surprise me, the last forty eight hours of angst had obviously brought feelings to a head and there didn't seem any point in Jimmi continuing if his heart wasn't in it. I Facebooked him to let him know I agreed with his decision.

Hi Jimmi, Jay said you don't want to play with OJ anymore, which is fine if you're not feeling it. Just wanted to thank you for all the fun times we had playing together and all your encouragement with my playing and help with the CD. You will always have a special place in my heart and music. See you soon. JX

    Jimmi messaged me back that it was nothing personal and he didn't want to upset anybody, but he wasn't enjoying it anymore, wasn't getting paid and in any case Outlaw Jones was more about mine and Jay's relationship as players and whatever else there was between us. We shared some Facebook hugs and I was glad Jimmi been straight and didn't I have a problem with any of it. He was right too; about OJ being more about me and Jay, and 'whatever else' there was between us, which still confused me. Ally had asked me about it the previous day when we had been chatting after the gig had finished and Jay had left.

    "So, what IS your relationship with Jay?" she had interjected suddenly.

    "We're just good friends," I said taken slightly back by the direct nature of her question.

    "Well, you should tell him. He has very strong feelings for you and reads every little sign from you as a possible signal that there may be hope for him."

    "I have told him, a number of times," I looked at my feet feeling awkward.

    "Well, he's not taking it on board and is always hoping there might be more."

"I know, but I don't want to stop seeing him, he's my best friend and my music partner."

"Well, maybe that's what you have to do for his sake. Sorry to be so blunt, he's a lovely guy and if you don't feel the same way about him as he does about you, then it might be best if you don't see him anymore."

I left shortly afterwards, mulling over what she had said. She had put into words what I had felt for a long time, but I thought I could have it all, Jay's friendship, love and music, without giving back the feelings that he wanted from me. I was due to go to the Gower Bluegrass festival with him the following weekend. It would be a year since we had been down there, when my retinae had detached for the first time. I had spent most of the festival weekend recovering, lying face down in the van on the consultant's instructions with Jay tenderly looking after me.

During that short time, I thought we had come to an understanding, and that we could stay close friends who had a special musical connection, however the last year had been a rocky road, punctuated by my unsteady walk down the friendship line and Jays accompanying mood swings. Still, we'd already arranged to go, and it looked like the weather was going to be fine. The Gower was beautiful and held happy memories for both of us and there would be lots of music. Surely everything would be fine?

It started well enough, with both of us in a good mood, which was just as well as we drove along the long diversion route caused by an accident. We stopped in the Vale of Rheidol, sitting in companionable silence as we ate our sandwiches looking out across the valley. "You know you can't say there isn't an 'us,'" Jay reflected after a while. I continued to stare into the distance but had to agree with what he said, there was comfortable familiarity about our relationship that went beyond friendship.

When we finally arrived at the heritage centre at Parkmill the organisers kindly squeezed us onto a small pitch, as we hadn't realised that all the campsites were full for the weekend and hadn't pre-booked anywhere to stay. I had just bought a new awning to attach to the van, which presented us with an intriguing puzzle to solve, despite having watched the assembly video prior to attempting to erect it. The video had been taken indoors and the tent unfolded and popped up like a Swiss army knife in about ten minutes, with two smiley men working together in perfect synchronicity to the accompanying music.

About an hour later a misshapen bagging awning had been attached to the van by myself, Jay and two friendly neighbours, Daryl and Roger. During the brief time I had spent with Roger, putting tent poles together, I had learnt a lot about his medical history and life philosophy.

"I always say apart from breathing you get a choice about everything in life, and it's up to you to make the most of it, so when the doctor told me I wouldn't walk again I took no notice of him and now I'm a park ranger," he concluded proudly.

He was up dressed in Country and Western gear, of bootlace tie, leather waistcoat and Stetson, and seemed unperturbed at having apparently got lost on route to the 'Hoedown'. Equally unnerved at finding herself at a Bluegrass festival, was his wife, who waved at us from their caravan door sporting a Tammy Wynette kind of look of cowboy boots and flowery dress. Roger waved back, and they left together in their finery for The Gower Inn, embarking on a journey of discovery as to what an evening session of Bluegrass held in a pub entailed. Earlier Roger had looked askance when I asked him if he played a musical instrument, but I felt sure he would have a good time at the session, even without a banjo or the prospect of any line dancing.

Shortly after Jay and I decided not to worry about what to do with the two left over tent poles and joined the revellers at the Gower Inn. There was no wind threatening to blow down the unsteady structure leaning against the van and although it was supposed to be a drive away awning, the compact nature of the vehicles parked in the field meant there would be little chance to move the van and test this theory. If we wanted to explore further than the field at Parkmill we would have to do it on foot. This was not a problem since there were lots of beautiful walks in the immediate vicinity, and we took the opportunity over the next few days to explore some of them.

As we wandered happily around on warm sandy beaches and swam in the blue sea, love was in the air, but it wasn't us. Huw, our friend from the Hurricane Hill Billies, had stepped out his van hand in hand with a new lady. We normally jammed with Huw and he was never seen far from his double bass, but this weekend it lay abandoned, as Huw wandered around starry eyed with other things on his mind.

I was cautious around Jay, remembering how close we had been the previous year and how dependent I had been on him. I sensed him looking back on that time with wistful fondness and I didn't want to upset him. The time was passing quite pleasantly and I wanted to hold on to our friendship, we had even talked about staying on for an extra day or two to explore some of the rest of the Gower. However, on Sunday morning the mood evaporated after Jay had had a bad night's sleep and awoke short tempered, snapping at me with sarcastic barbs and making me feel defensive. Giving up smoking a few days earlier had probably not helped matters, but by lunch time his mood seemed to have improved and he apologised for his early morning grouchiness and sat happily munching a pasty in the sun. I wasn't hungry and picked up my violin to practice.

A few minutes later Jay put his pasty down and joined me on his guitar. We played a couple of tunes before the warm sunshine inspired me to play *Summertime*. I turned to him at the point he normally sang and he flashed a look of annoyance at me. He hadn't finished a mouthful of food he'd been chewing and started to sing still struggling to swallow the crumbs in his mouth. He then decided to sing trying out the effect of several different accents before settling on a Yorkshire one. I stopped in exasperation with him ridiculing a song I loved.

"What!" he snapped at me.

"You're making it sound stupid; I don't want to play it anymore."

"Well what do you expect? I've got a mouthful of food and I don't like Summertime anyway, never have done. It's only because you like it that I play it, it's just an over hyped show song," he scorned.

I stared at him feeling hurt. I thought *Summertime* was a great song, capturing the mood of the season perfectly with its lyrics and tune, and I felt patronised that Jay had played it so many times with me without having appreciated that he didn't share the same sentiment.

"I didn't realise you were still eating and I didn't know you didn't like *Summertime.*"

"Well that's just typical of you, you don't notice anything."

Suddenly it seemed like we had nothing in common, and although I didn't want it to end on a bad note, musically or personally, I had no desire to prolong the holiday any longer than necessary. I put down my violin.

"I think we should pack up and leave once we've seen the Jaywalkers."

I went back to the van to tidy up and once he had finished lunch Jay helped me. As I compressed my sleeping bag into a small bundled I thought back to what Ally had said to me and realised I had asked too much of Jay to come to the Gower. It only took a little tiredness to wear down his bravery, and his frustration with our relationship started to envelope him like a dark cloud. The feelings we had shared three years previously could not be recaptured, and although I had told Jay that things might be different after I left my husband and sorted my life out, they weren't. It was now eighteen months since I'd been separated and I had no desire to entangle myself in another relationship, with Jay or anyone else.

We drove back quietly while I reflected on my friendship with Jay which was always on my terms, terms that were proving increasingly detrimental to his happiness. For his sake I had to step away and forgo the things I valued most in our relationship, his companionship and the music. We arrived back to where Jay had left his car and transferred his stuff into it and I took a deep breath.

"I don't think I should come over to Dolwen anymore, I need some space."

Jay also took a deep breath.

"Okay" he said and we shared a brief hug.

By the time I'd got home Jay had already sent me a text

This doesn't feel right. Maybe we should talk about it?

I replied, *You choose the right stone; things will feel better after a night sleep X*

The stone I was referring to was a small polished gem Jay had chosen in the small gift shop in Heritage Centre. There had been a selection of stones, each supposedly representing different qualities and I had bought some and suggested to Jay that he choose one for himself. His stone was supposed to hold the quality of courage and maybe it was the gem or something else, but Jay managed to steel himself and his messages dried up.

A week or so later he sent me a text asking if I'd still like to play music with him. I replied, "Of course," but thought at the moment it would be difficult for both of us, and although I missed playing with him, I was happy to jam along by myself to backing tracks. As Jay had astutely pointed out all the things I enjoyed doing, running, single handed sailing and writing, were solitary pursuits, and it seemed like my music was following the same route.

Gradually I got use not having regular contact with Jay. It was strange not having someone I could call on and rely on anymore, no one to jam with and no one exchange a good night text with, but I needed to know we could see each other without falling back into old habits. I knew we would meet up soon, as Ally was having a birthday party at Shady Grove, and perhaps meeting on neutral territory would be the best way forward. Jimmi would also be going, and I wondered whether viewing Shady Grove as "neutral territory" for the three of us was wistful thinking on my part. It was the place Jimmi most wanted to be, and aspired to return to, the place to where I had escaped from the problems of married life, and the place where Jay and I had been closest. Would the old farmhouse ensnare us with its sentimental magic or could we break the spell and move on?

...

As we sat around the table around the table, I felt a surge of warmth for the people around me and it wasn't just the extra chillies Sam had put in the chicken curry he had cooked, it felt really good to see everyone. Jay and I were somewhat cautious around each other, but it was okay, and Jimmi looked happier and more relaxed than I'd seen him for a while. He was chatting to Steve about the Snake Inn in Derbyshire, a place, where several of us had had previous experiences. I was thinking about the foul night many years before when I had stumbled into its sanctuary, lost on a moorland expedition with a group of young apprentice coal miners. Steve had already turned his attention to his adventures a little further down the Snake Pass, and the town of Glossop. He paused in his tale and Jimmi took the opportunity to casually interject, "I once met a witch in Glossop."

The thought of this unusual encounter caught my attention and dragged me from my reminisces, actually I don't know why I was surprised by what he had said because Jimmi was the sort of person who would meet a witch in Glossop.

"How do you know she was a witch?" I asked.

"Because she told me, and I knew she was anyway, she had green eyes and dark curly hair." He paused reflecting on the meeting, "She wanted me to go to Egypt with her," he continued. There was general laughter as his story was beginning to seem a little over stretched. But I was immediately captivated by the thought of the witch who wanted to go to Egypt. Who was she and why did she want to go to Egypt?

As the evening went on I couldn't get her out of my head. We'd gone over to Sam's to listen to him playing piano. Jimmi had just done some recording with him and his friends, Izzy on vocals, and Twm on double bass. I crept through the connecting larder door into Sam's house, which was always felt a bit like going through the wardrobe into Narnia. It was even more like that as an elevated wooden bed had been built in the room which used a thick tree branch as a supporting leg. Sam was sitting playing at his shiny, black, Scheidmayer baby grand piano and in the absence of Twm, Jimmi was playing electric bass.

In between admiring Sam's playing and marvelling at how Izzy was singing to a rather random sounding tune, I was thinking about the Witch, I was fascinated by her, feeling she held the key to something significant in my life. I felt compelled to learn more about her and turned to Steve.

"Steve using regression therapy is it possible to connect with someone I've never known?"

"I don't know," he frowned, "I suppose in theory yes. We all leave part of our self in the spirit world so we are all connected."

I continued to mull it over as I left the party in the small hours and drove through the gate and down the small dark lane from Shady Grove. Somehow I would find the Witch who went to Egypt and learn why she was important to me.

Chapter 6. The Witch

In the past, men created witches: now they create mental patients. (Thomas Szasz)

The Witch looked up over the old stone wall and across to the bleak hill in the distance, something had disturbed her concentration and unsettled her. She paused for a while, scanning the sky line, before returning her gaze to the vegetable patch in front of her, where she was kneeling digging out some old potato plants. The skin on her hands was dry and cracked from her hard labour, dirt stuffed down her finger nails. She got up, brushed the mud from her palms and pushed back her dark curly hair, then picked up her tools and clomped down the garden path in her Wellington boots. Stopping at the garden shed she swapped her footwear for a pair of clogs and, with a clang, put the bucket and fork she had been using in a dusty corner. She continued down the path, which led to an old cottage, pushed open the front door and went inside.

It was late afternoon, and although outside the sinking autumn sun sharpened the cloud edges, giving them purple glow, only a grey light seeped through the dirty window panes. The Witch felt around in her cardigan pocket, pulled out a box of matches and struck one, the flare of the match reflecting back in her green eyes. Protecting the flame with her hand she used it to light a large candle, left stuck in white icicles of grease on the wooden kitchen table. A feeble glow spread out from the burning wick, just giving enough illumination for her to make her way across the stone flags to the sink standing in the corner. She turned the stiff tap on and washed her hands with a nail brush and a large block of soap. The brown water spiralled down the plug hole, and when it eventually ran clean she turned the tap off with a squeak, drying her hands on a rough towel hanging from a hook.

Picking up a battered kettle from the floor she plonked it on top of the range with a bang, causing water to slop from the spout, hissing as it dropped onto the hot metal. Her chores finally done, she sank down into a shabby arm chair in front of the fireplace, a plump rush of air gushing from the cushions as her capacious backside landed. The embers in the grate glowed weakly and she leant forward and stabbed them with a poker until some lazy flames licked around the coals. Satisfied with the blaze she leant back into the chair. With a sigh closed her eyes, the lines on her face relaxed and the soft flesh of her cheeks drooped down towards her mouth. She breathed heavily, apparently asleep.

"You took your time," she said crossly, taking me by surprise.

"Sorry, I didn't know about you until recently and didn't know how to get here," I tried to excused myself.

"Really? I've been waiting years and if you had actually looked you would have found me."

"Who are you?"

"The Witch who went to Egypt."

"Yes, I know, but what's your name?"

"Eleanor."

"Are you really a witch?"

"I guess some people might call me that, but I don't have a wand, a pointy hat, or fly around on a broom stick. Of all the notions held about witches the broomstick one is probably the most ridiculous. Can you imagine anything more uncomfortable than trying to fly sitting on one, or more impractical? Arriving at your destination with your hair all windblown and flies stuck to your face, besides which, for all their agility, how would Ping and Pong be able to stay on it?"

"Who are Ping and Pong?"

"The cats," she nodded to the armchair next to her where two Siamese cats lay basking in the heat of the fire.

"Well, I can see there would be problems with broomstick travel, so how do you normally get around?"

"I mind travel."

"Mind travel?"

"What you're doing now. Are you stopping long?"

"I don't think so, I only got here with the help of Steve and he's going soon to see Jimmi."

"Ah yes, Jimmi!"

Suddenly I could see Jimmi; he had a drink in his hand and was scanning the crowd of people in the room who were intermittently lit up by the stage lighting. The music was very loud, with a thumping base. He laughed and shouted loudly to the person next to him, it was Eleanor, who also laughed, and then the crowd and noise faded away. She smiled ruefully, "I think we would have had fun in Egypt."

"So, you never went there?"

"Not yet, I just asked Jimmi to get him to say the line, that's how I met you."

"Eh?"

"I knew you wouldn't be able to resist the intrigue of finding out about me. Jimmi meeting a witch wouldn't be enough to drawn you in, but the Witch who went to Egypt is far more interesting and a great title for a book, don't you think? Even given that its brilliant mystery to solve, it's taken you a long time to get to the point where you finally came looking for me; violins, Jay, marriage breakdowns, etcetera, etcetera."

"Why am I here?"

"To learn a bit more about living, if you want."

"And your part in this?"

"I'm your guide," Eleanor sighed impatiently, as if it was something she'd told me many times. "I'm here to help you to appreciate the ride more; learn some more about yourself and other dimensions, introduce you to some new friends, and in general spread a little magic. I got Jay to give you a book to help explain."

"The Afterlife of Billy Fingers?"

"Yes, what did you think of it?"

"Well," I reflected, "for me spiritualism is self-evident, and therefore there must be an afterlife, but I found that version of events a bit over egged."

"For you maybe," she smiled, "but spiritualism covers a whole spectrum of possibilities. I know you're sceptical but you will see that I'm here for your benefit. The more open minded you are the more you'll learn."

"Great, I need to learn the saxophone."

"I didn't mean a musical instrument," the Witch sounded exasperated, "anyway, what happened to the cello?"

"It's not happening for me, I'm not feeling it. I need something I can breathe into, something I can fill my spirit with," I said trying to get the Witch on my side. "I need to do it, and don't want to have to practice for years to get to a reasonable standard."

"Well that's what it takes, years of practice and dedication, you know that. There are no short cuts for practice, but you won't be starting from zilch, you already have the musicality and experience you've gained over the last few years, you just need to learn the technicalities of the instrument to direct it."

"Well it's still going to take ages. Can't you find a spirit who plays the sax and get them to guide me?"

"No."

"Can't you help me in anyway? Please? Music is a passionate expression for me, a way of connecting with my soul," I tried to plead my case as the Witch started to fade.

She came back into focus and spoke, "You're right, so I will give you some help, but in a way I think fit. To start with here's some advice, are you listening carefully?"

"Yes," what was this, I thought, *'Listen with Mother'*? I stopped breathing I was concentrating so hard. Eleanor spoke in a calm, serene voice, I thought I could her angels singing; "The first thing is to savour each note," the chorus got louder, "secondly don't make the same mistakes with Jimmi as you did with Jay, and finally" she snapped irritability, "stop rushing around so much, you're missing the moment and giving me a headache." The music stopped and there was a sharp screech like a needle being dragged across a record.

"Is that it?" I said disappointed, I was expecting at least something equivalent to the Ten Commandments, and what did she mean about Jimmi and Jay?

"That's it," she said firmly, "except you don't need Steve to find me, just relax, look around, and I'll be there," then she was gone and I was back in the room with Steve.

…

Not long after my first encounter with the Witch I was on the train to Shrewsbury, on a mission to hire a saxophone from a shop called the Windband. The idea of playing sax had come to me the same time as I'd considering the cello, but I thought I might find the cello easier, so had gone with that idea first. As I'd struggled with the cello, playing a sax had loomed larger in my mind, maybe I just needed to try something completely different. Designed by a Belgian instrument maker, Adolphe Sax, in 1840, his idea had been to produce an instrument that combined the agility of woodwind with the projection of brass. Its' versatility is such that it is equally adept at producing a loud, raunchy sound, as soft melancholic sadness, making it popular in all kinds of music, from marching bands to chamber music, as well as being a signature sound of Jazz.

There are four basic saxophones, soprano, alto, tenor and baritone and after a bit of research I had decided I would like to try a soprano sax, just like I'd heard Muttley play when he'd been visiting the previous summer. It was the smallest of the four saxes and certainly groovy; I wondered how hard it would be to play.

It was only 9.30am and I was already tired, lack of sleep, extra hours at work and worries about my children had left me drained, added to which my computer had blown up and I'd been struggling to set up a new one, I'd strained a calf muscle and couldn't run, my bike was broken and I couldn't bike, and I was concerned about Jay. I'd had little contact with him over the last few weeks and I hoped he was alright. No sooner had I had that thought than a text pinged up, it was Jay.

"Hi. I know any relationship we had is long over but I thought I should tell you I met someone. A hippy chick in fact!"

I felt a range of emotions, surprise, relief, happiness for him, a tinge of sadness and nostalgia, for all the good times we'd shared together, and finality, knowing that there was no going back. I texted him to wish him well and quite a few miles clacked by on the rails before I could focus on the work in front of me, the annoying lady shouting down her phone to a friend somewhere in Derbyshire, helped. I looked at the passenger sitting opposite me and we rolled our eyes, screwed our headphones in and turned the volume up. Finally we arrived in Shrewsbury.

I allowed myself to go into a bit of a shopping frenzy before finally making my way to the music shop, stopping about half a dozen passers-by in my route finding efforts, and arriving somewhat hot and sweaty. I dumped my shopping on the floor and stripped off my coat and jumper. The shop assistant, Bethan, invited me into the back room and unpacked the straight soprano that I was thinking of hiring. Straight soprano's look more like a clarinet, than a sax, and are preferred by many modern players. She tighter up the ligature around the reed and gave me the mouth piece.

"Have you ever played a sax before?"

"No, I've never played a wind instrument of any kind, well except a recorder as a kid at primary school."

"Well that will help," she smiled.

"That was about forty five years ago," I said dubiously.

I blew into the mouth piece, trying to remember the advice I'd seen on You Tube. After an immense amount of effort a strangulated note came out. Like one of those party whistles, it wasn't pleasant. Bethan attached the mouth piece to the neck and handed me the whole instrument, I blew into it without much better results. I tried pressing down the keys, each note took a greater amount of exertion to blow, and by the time I reached the bottom I thought my head was going to explode. I suddenly realised I'd hardly had anything to eat that day and I was dizzy and in danger of passing out on the floor.

"This is taking far more energy than I thought," I gasped to Bethan, "I can't imagine being able to play this, I have to take a breath for every note and I think I'm about to faint."

"Well the soprano sax is the hardest sax to get a note out, simply because it's got the smallest mouth piece, alto and tenor are easier because they have bigger mouth pieces."

"Can I try an alto?"

"Sure," and she brought out a surprisingly compact bag. I was impressed. One of the reasons I hadn't really considered an alto was because I thought it would be cumbersome to travel with, but the carrying case wasn't much bigger than my violin case.

I attached the alto to the neck strap I was wearing, it was a lot heavier than the soprano, and I wouldn't have wanted to just support it with just my arms. I blew into it and a soft note came out, which encouragingly sounded like the sort of noise a saxophone should make. It soon became apparent I was getting a lot better results than with the soprano, even managing to play several notes before I ran out of breath. I experimented for a while before turning to Bethan.

"On second thoughts I think I'd like to hire an alto sax, I never liked Kenny G anyway."

She laughed and packed up the instrument. I bought some extra reeds, a cleaning kit, and then I was on my way, the black tubby case swinging by my side.

Once back home I couldn't wait to try it again and I assembled all the pieces and stood in front of the mirror, so I could see that my fingers were placed on the right buttons. There seemed to be so many knobs and levers sticking out it was easy to press the wrong thing. I spent some time fiddling with the neck strap, trying to get the mouth piece to sit at the correct height so that it rested on my bottom lip, without compressing it too much. As I began to play a variety of uncontrolled sounds came out, and I rapidly discovered the most crucial part of playing any wind instrument, the embouchure.

Embouchure, from the French word 'bouche', meaning mouth, is the way the lips are used to form a seal around the mouth piece and vibrate the reed. It is responsible for the quality of the tone and intonation of the sound, and looking online there seemed to be endless discussions and opinions about how it should be done. Ultimately there seemed to be no definitive answer, because people's faces are all shaped differently, and musical expression requires subtle changes in the embouchure needed, anyway.

I tried to tune it, but I couldn't make any sense of what the dial on the tuner I was using was telling me. Basic tuning of the sax is adjusted by how far the mouth piece is pushed onto the cork attachment point at the end of the neck, with embouchure responsible for fine tuning. The conical shape of the brass tube mean there are tuning 'tendencies' in the design, as the attachment of the mouth piece doesn't allow the tapering to continue at the neck, so just because one note is in tune it doesn't mean the rest will be. Added to that problem, the notes of the upper register have a more flexible pitch than the lower ones, and the speed and intensity of a breath can also alter the pitch of a note, as well as the quality of the reed.

Even given all of those difficulties I couldn't understand what was going on, I sounded in tune but was playing a different note to the button I was pressing. For the moment I decided not to worry about it and just play. After a while I improved slightly, but my lips and lungs soon tired and the law of diminishing returns kicked in, more strange notes came out than good ones, and I had to stop. It was going to take a while to get fit enough to play the sax for longer periods and I moved on to the next mysterious problem, which was the process of drying the sax out before I put it away.

I had read that if I didn't dry the sax out "gross" things would grow inside it. The pads on the buttons would absorb the moisture, causing them to shrink as they dried, eventually leaking air. I had bought a special pull through rag to do the job and when I tipped up the sax to grab the weighted chord at the other end, a load of spit dripped out, it was really disgusting. I wondered whether the amount of spit I had produced was normal and how quickly I would dehydrate if I kept on playing. It was clearly the least charming aspect of playing the sax, but apart from that I loved it. Its amazing capacity for expression and nuance seemed limitless; I just had to learn to harness its potential and practice as much as I could. I had read somewhere that the best way to get good quick was to practice at least an hour every day, and that was what I intended to do.

The following morning I picked it up again and once I had tired, headed for the supermarket to do the weekly shop. I appeared to have run out of everything and was trying to balance various boxes and bags in my trolley at the check-out, when a familiar voice with a Scouse accent cut in.

"You need a hand with that?"

It was Jimmi; he looked drained and was standing holding a packet of fish and carton of milk, appearing rather uncertain with what to do with them.

"Yes please, what are you doing here?" It wasn't exactly his local shop, and it felt like more than a coincidence meeting him. I found that whenever people were on my mind, even sub-consciously, I bumped into them, or they contacted me. Recently the delicate balancing act of Jimmi's love life had gone horribly wrong, and I had been wondering how he was getting on.

"I stayed at Shady Grove last night and I'm not sure what I'm going to do now," he said shuffling the packets of food around in his hands.

"You want to come back for some lunch?"

"Yeah, that would be great," he looked relieved and we took the shopping back to the car.

"Your back tyre's flat," he pointed out.

"Thanks, I think you might have just saved my life, I hadn't noticed," I said gratefully.

"Think you might have just saved mine," he said ruefully.

"Guess our meeting was fortuitous for both of us then," I smiled.

I put my trolley back and took the car round to the garage where Jimmi put some air in the tyre before we drove back to the house. I put some lunch on the table and we chatted. It felt like déjà vu, Jimmi had been through the same scenario before with the same two women, Jane and Tess. It had been going on for a while and I assumed that Jimmi knew what he was doing, but apparently not. He had just been digging himself a deeper and deeper hole.

I remembered back to the dark evening a couple of years previously when I had found him in tears at Shady Grove. I was as bewildered as Jimmi as to how it had all happened again. Jimmi blamed Jay for the final show down, feeling that he had not only "dropped the bomb", but had been self-righteous about it and taken pleasure in Jimmi's downfall. Jimmi was so angry with Jay he felt he couldn't go back to Dolwen, which was why he was sleeping on the couch at Shady Grove and looking for somewhere else to live.

As Jimmi went on and on about Jay, I began to wondered if Jay's disaffection with our relationship had made him less than diplomatic in what he had said, and therefore whether I was also partly to blame for the mess. I added it to the mountain of guilt I was carrying, but however blame was apportioned there was no doubt that Jimmi had committed the offence. There seemed no point on dwelling on it any longer, and I picked my sax up, trying to change the subject.

"Suits you better than the fiddle," said Jimmi approvingly, after I'd had a play.

"Maybe," I said shrugging my shoulders, "I've only had it a day, but I really like it. I'll have to do something about this neck strap, though, its killing me," I said taking it off. "Fancy a walk?"

"Okay," he agreed, and we set off. As we passed the parked car outside the door and headed on up the steep slope he started to look a bit worried.

"You'll be fine," I reassured him, "it flattens off just up there," I pointed vaguely to the brow of the hill. After a few yards his breathing had increase to a rather alarming level, and it was my turn to feel concerned. Jimmi had a heart problem and wasn't in the best of health, maybe I'd been over ambitious.

"Just take your time," I advised nervously.

He made it, and I relaxed as we turned down the hill and he began to enjoy the views. We managed a small circle of the village and I rustled up a roast chicken in celebration. Jimmi seemed a little happier after the meal and I could see him getting comfortable on the couch.

"I think you should go back to Dolwen," I encourage him gently, "if only to get a change of clothes." Reluctantly he agreed and went off into the dark night, sending me a text that he had arrived back safely. I felt relieved until the next day when he messaged me that he was back at Shady Grove again, having flown into a rage after discovering Jay had posted on Facebook he was in a relationship. Jay said he had already told Jimmi about it, but I guess it just hit him at a bad time. I wondered how long Jimmi would hold the grudge, and how long the folks at Shady Grove would let him stay. As I looked at the pictures of Jay and Jimmi on my wall, playing their guitars in happier times, I felt tears prick my eyes wondering how it had all gone so wrong.

The next day at work, I got a text from Jay, asking me if I knew why Jimmi was looking for somewhere else to live. Briefly I explained that Jimmi thought he had been interfering and judgemental in his affairs. Jay thought they had talked it all out and reached an understanding, but there seemed little common ground between the two of them. When Jimmi found out that Jay knew he was at Shady Grove, he jumped into his car and drove up north. I got home to receive another series of messages from him about how Jay had done him wrong, but I thought Jimmi should take some responsibility, and messaged him back to say so, before I finally went to bed.

The following morning I was having a very weird dream that I was getting married to my husband. The ceremony was really odd; the congregation wasn't dressed right and were disco dancing to the hymns. Some of the young lads went onto the roof of the church and started chucking boulders down onto people as they left. My son's alarm was going off. My sons alarm was going off! The noise entered my dreams and I quickly rolled over and fell out of bed. It wasn't very far but I hit my head on the side table, bit my cheek, cut my chin and knocked over a glass of water. I found the side light and sat dazed and wet on the floor, trying to find out where the blood was coming from. I never fallen out of bed in my entire life and speculated if I'd reached the time of life where I needed cot sides.

It was six thirty; I cleared up the mess and sat holding a tissue to my chin, trying to stop it bleeding. I had a headache and wondered if I had concussion. After getting my son off to school, I took some paracetamol and had a cup of tea while I picked up my phone messages. There was a volley of communications from Jimmi, who hadn't appreciated my unsympathetic bedtime text. His angry words added to the banging going on in my head and left me feeling drained. The day limped by, I made myself do some sax, but the noise was loud and my cheek hurt where I had bitten it. I was slumped on the settee in the afternoon when the phone went and I picked up an international call from a man with an Indian accent from Microsoft, saying they'd had some problems with my Windows 8 spreading viruses on their network. Since I'd just purchased a lap top a couple of weeks previously I wasn't suspicious, but then he wanted access to my computer to sort it out.

"How do I know you are who you say you are?" I asked warily.

"Just get your license number and I will prove it to you. This is very bad for Microsoft and we will have to block your computer if we don't clean it up."

"Block my computer? I've only just bought it," I said indignantly.

The banging in my head grew louder as the threats continued and the only way to stop it was to slam the phone down. He rang back and left a long and angry message about what was going to happen to me if I didn't pick the phone up. He phoned a third time and issued his final threat, "You will be blocked for the rest of your life," he hissed malevolently. I was passed caring.

I phoned the man who sold me the laptop, who confirmed it was a scam. In my weakened state I nearly fell for it and speculated how many vulnerable victims were conned by such an intimidating experience. A less than perfect day was topped by an evening phone call from Jimmi, who was seething with rage on a couch somewhere in Garstang, and spent about half an hour telling me again how Jay had ruined his life. I let him rant on until he calmed down a bit, and then said I had to go. I wondered if he'd ever come back, and if not, how Jay would pay his mortgage. Maybe it wasn't happening and was just part of the strange dream I'd been having.

…

The next morning my head felt better, which was just as well as it was a work day. I had got through the mornings' list of patients without much drama and was expecting more of the same in the afternoon. The first patient who came in was a gentleman walking with the aid of a stick. I had seen him the previous week and suggested that he might benefit from using a stick to support his arthritic knees and offered him a trusty NHS one. He turned this down, telling me he had a good one at home, so I asked him to bring it in so I could check it was the right height for him.

"Wow, that looks a solid piece of wood," I said admiring the substantial looking stick.

"Yes my best friend made it for me," he said proudly, "he did a really good job."

"Looks like it. It just needs a ferrule on the end to stop it slipping on the ground; I'll put one on for you."

I got a ferrule out of the draw and placed it on the floor so I could press the end of the stick into it. It was quite tight and I had to press down firmly on the top. Suddenly there loud 'crack' and the handle snapped. As I headed towards the floor with the handle still in my hand my first thought was how amazingly strong I was, followed by "Oh sh*t I've just broken his best friends stick." I picked the two pieces up and we both gaped at them, speechless. I put them together, hoping they would somehow magically glue but they didn't, then I juggled them around for a while in my hands, uncertain what to do before putting them behind my back and gazing at the ceiling, hoping he would forget about the incident. When I looked back down again he was still staring at me in an apparent state of shock.

"Err, maybe you should try one of ours," I said and I quickly disappeared into the cupboard to examine the broken pieces. The maker had constructed it using a small piece of dowel to attach the head of the stick to the body. From its inherent design fault it was evident that I wasn't superwoman and I wasn't surprised it had broken. I got a reliable 'all in one' NHS stick from the stack in the corner and returned offering it to him with a bright smile, "Here this should do the job." He starred at it, unmoved by my generosity, it wasn't hand carved, it wasn't shiny, and it definitely hadn't been made by his best friend.

I handed him back the broken pieces, deciding not to point out the weakness of the design. "Maybe you could fix it and hang it up your wall? It's nice to look at but ours might be safer to walk with." Unsurprisingly he didn't look impressed by my suggestion, and left clutching the precious bits of wood in his spare hand. A week later he returned, walking with the offending stick, "I got my friend to fix it," he said defiantly.

"Great!" I said through gritted teeth, and decided to drop the subject; sometimes well-meaning advice is powerless unless the recipient is in the right frame of mind to receive it. I had definitely come to that point myself. After a couple of weeks of trying to learn the sax, I decided I needed to get some help and someone to explain to me a few basics; like why different notes were coming out to the ones I was playing would be a good start. After a bit of research on the web I found a gentleman living about an hour away and arranged to see him a few days later. When he opened the door to welcome me I found the mental picture I had of him turned out to be entirely accurate. Terry was definitely a teacher of the old school type. There was no hurrying him and I was so desperate to learn I had to sit on my hands to avoid leaping off the chair and wringing the information from him. When he finally paused from his careful instructions to look for some ancient saxophone book, I took my opportunity.

"So, how do you tune it? I know you pull the mouth piece in and out but the note is way off what my tuner says."

"That's because it's a transposing instrument, which means the played note doesn't correspond to the same note as concert pitch instruments, like a piano. It's an E flat alto sax, so when you play a C its E flat on the piano, three semi tones above."

What! It all seemed like a dastardly conspiracy by the music world to confuse people like me who were already confused enough by musical theory. Later I found out there were historical reasons for it, to make it easier to switch between instruments of the same family, but it seemed like another obstacle to overcome. It also made life slightly more complicated when joining in a session with other instruments playing in concert pitch, like guitars, because I would always be playing in a different key.

I arrived back home feeling dizzy, but soon couldn't resist getting my sax out again and practicing my scales, playing C, which was really A. When I got down to the bottom C, there was some horrible squeaking, and the D was making a strange rumbling sound. I tried over and over again, getting more tired and distraught. It had been fine previously and I decided I must have damaged it in transit and phoned Terry to ask his advice; he wasn't in so I left a message. After more futile efforts I decided to put it away and take it back to Shrewsbury as soon as possible. Meanwhile I guess I could play it without using the bottom notes. I took the neck off and tipped it up to clean it, there was sure gonna be a lot of spit in it after all my efforts. The cleaning rag fell out and the reason for my problems became apparent. I remembered how I'd hurriedly stuffed it in the end of the horn, when I'd packed up at Terry's, and I didn't know whether to laugh or cry. It was even more dull than the mistake I'd made in the first few days, when after half an hour of very unpleasant sounds I'd discovered I'd put the reed on upside down.

I phoned Terry back and left another garbled message to cancel the previous one I'd left and decided I didn't have the energy to go to the monthly pub session and meet Jay and Matt. I hadn't seen Jay since the last session but he seemed to be doing fine, Jimmi had returned to Dolwen a few days previously and I speculated about what sort of truce the guys had come to. I hoped the reappearance of Jimmi's usual Facebook account, which he had closed down, and that he had accepted Jay as a friend on it, was a positive sign. I felt my spirits lift when I saw the apparently good news, and decided to go for a run along the beach, and test my injured calf out properly.

It was a very still and mild morning and as I ran along the sand I marvelled at the sky, which had divided its self into a milky blue base topped by dark, silver layers of cloud. The Witch appeared and ran past me wearing a dayglow head band with matching leg warmers, and black Lycra leggings. I thought she should exhibit more caution when wearing lycra but she disdainfully dismissed my thoughts and pulled away into the distance, not letting me catch up until I had admitted she was fitter than me, whatever her shape.

"I think you should go and see Jay," she said running backwards with ease, not even puffing.

"Really?" I gasped, hoping she would trip over and face plant in the sand.

"Yes, really. Have a nice day." She disappeared into the distance doing a series of cartwheels and flick flacks, her acrobatics making her resemble a bouncing beach ball, blown along by the wind.

A few days later I was driving near to Dolwen and called Jay on my mobile; he was on his way back from a shopping expedition and cheerily told me to drop by. I arrived before him. Jimmi was also out and I stood in the kitchen remembering all the times I had shared with them, the hours of music and recording our CD, meals around the table, chatting and laughing together, the warmth and friendship. Suddenly the door banged and Jay walked in looking happy and relaxed.

We had a cup of tea and a laugh, like old times, but with a clear boundary between us, and none of the angst. The following week, when he was over my way, he came to see me and we had a play for the first time in about two months. The old tunes we had played together for years felt fresh again and I hoped we could still share some musical fun in the future. I hadn't yet revealed my new interest in the saxophone to him and wondered whether he would be part of that adventure, or whether I was about to embark on a new musical journey without him.

Chapter 7. Bird

They teach you there's a boundary line to music. But, man, there's no boundary line to art. (Charlie Parker)

I thought I'd call by to see the Witch and see if she had any more advice for me on playing the sax and found myself in her garden. It was a warm lazy day and there was of no sign of Eleanor, just a black man sitting on the garden bench holding a saxophone. He put it to his lips and began to play *Summertime* and the soft notes dripped from his horn like honey. I recognised him; it was Charlie Parker, also known as Bird. There are various stories about how he acquired his nickname, one of which is that he was in vehicle, on his way to a gig, which hit a yardbird. Charlie got the bird and a feast, but maybe the name stuck because Charlie played as free as a bird, some feeling he was the greatest Jazz saxophonist ever to have lived, perhaps the greatest Jazz player there has ever been, due to his extraordinary improvisation skills and impact in changing the course of Jazz history with his contribution to the development of Bebop.

For the moment he was playing a straight version of *Summertime*, his clear tone wrapping sweetly around the notes. I could also hear strings playing in the background, sounding similar to his recording, *Charlie Parker with Strings*, and I looked up to see a shimmering orchestra on the grass hill behind the garden wall. Above the garden wall Eleanor floated by playing a violin, she was wearing a black cape which spilled out behind her in the slip stream she was generating. Determined to impress she reversed the manoeuver, whilst making a long sweep with her bow and doing an exaggerated vibrato. She was really hamming it up.

I turned away from the disconcerting image, concentrating my attention on Charlie. There was a golden light where the notes rose from his horn, and a bird hovered on the updraft created by the melody. The bird looked like a kittiwake, and with the subtlest of movements from its wing feathers, it held its position on the musical breeze. Charlie finished the tune, and the golden light and the bird faded away.

"That was beautiful," I said admiringly to him.

He turned to me and spoke in a slow American drawl, *"When I first heard music, I thought it should be very clean, very precise. Something that people could understand, something that was beautiful,"* he smiled and was gone.

Eleanor landed jauntily beside me on the lawn. "Thought you might like to meet Charlie and asked him to call by, then I thought what the heck and invited the whole orchestra too. What, do you think of my violin playing?"

"Err" I wasn't sure what to say, because I'd found her aeronautics very distracting, on top of which I felt the strings were a bit saccharine against the clarity of the saxophone. I decided to change the subject, "Is it hard to play the violin when you're flying?" I asked innocently.

"Only when you hit turbulence, you should try it. How's the sax going anyway? See, I kindly got rid of you cello for you so you wouldn't get diverted."

"Oh, thanks, thought it must be your doing." When I had gone to work the week after I'd hired my sax, my colleague, Janey, had said she was looking for a cello for her husband's birthday. The deal was quickly done, unfortunately the lovely Gunter and I were going to have to part company, but as I'd already fallen in love with sax I realised there was no way I had the time to learn the cello as well.

"You need all the time you can get," Eleanor read my thoughts, "took Charlie thousands of hours to sound the way he does."

"Yes, I love his sound, he really feels it."

"Here's his story," she said passing me a bound book with a golden embossed bird on the front, which looked like the kittiwake I had seen riding the musical updraft from Charlie's horn. I open the cover and turn the pages of his life.

Charlie was born in Kansas City in 1920 at the right time and in the right place for an aspiring Jazz player. Kansas City was a railroad town which came alive at night with the drinking, gambling and music of over fifty night clubs. It was the time of prohibition, often said to have been the United States government's "great gift" to Jazz, as clubs and bars sold illicit alcohol and drew their customers in with the reputation of the musicians that worked for them.

Charlie showed an early interest in music, joining the school band, and his mother bought him a saxophone. While she worked nights, Charlie was sneaking out of the house to listen to the music spilling out on to the streets from the local Jazz clubs like the Reno. Here, musicians like Count Basie might play the whole night through. The long hours of performance engendering all sorts of musical creativity, while a young Charlie Parker listened and dreamed of becoming part of it.

By fifteen Charlie had left school to pursue his musical ambitions. Early experiences of playing with other musicians were humiliating; one time when he got up to play *I got Rhythm* he was laughed off the stage when he couldn't switch key to follow what the rest of the band was playing. Another night he was waiting, along with other hopeful musicians, in the back alley behind the Reno club for a chance to play with the Basie band. He got his opportunity but the drummer, Jo Jones, wasn't impressed and threw a cymbal at him, forcing a chastened Charlie to leave. He took the hurt and used it to hone his skills, spending the next few years practicing long hours; however there was also another obsession taking over his life. On his the way to a gig one night he was involved in a serious car accident, ending up in hospital with a broken back and ribs. He was given morphine for the pain and by the time he returned home from hospital he was hooked on heroin.

I saw Charlie alone in a dimly lit bedroom sitting next to a table laid out with the 'works' needed for shooting up, slamming, banging, digging, mainlining, whatever you want to call it. Beads of sweat fleck his brow as he concentrates on some brown liquid in a spoon, which he gently heats by holding a match underneath the bowl. He blows out the match, carefully putting the spoon down, and then picks up a syringe, using it to draw up the substance from the spoon. Next he wraps his tie tightly around the top of his arm, pumping his fist until the vein stands out, extends his arm, and sticks the needle in, slowly squeezing the plunger down and releasing its contents into his blood. He can barely contain himself, but the rush to his brain only takes seconds, as it becomes rapidly flooded with the morphine binding onto to the opiate receptors lying in wait.

He gasps and draws his head back, closing his eyes, nodding; for the moment nothing else matters but the warmth and ecstasy cascading through his body. *Golden Brown, texture like sun, lays me down with my mind she runs, throughout the night, no need to fight, never a frown, with Golden Brown.* Nothing else matters until he needs to score again.

While the car crash probably contributed to Charlie becoming an addict, there was another more beneficial spin off; with the insurance money he received he bought a brand new Selmer saxophone. Soon he was getting regular work and improving his performance with the advice of other Jazz musicians he met, especially Buster Smith, who helped him develop a brighter tone and taught him the technique of double tonguing, enabling him to play much quicker tempo. When Buster left for New York, eighteen year old Charlie followed him.

In New York Charlie was mixing and jamming with many outstanding musicians and it was during this period, in particular from obsessively playing the song *Cherokee,* he discovered that he could improvise much more freely when following the harmonic arrangement, rather than the melodic line of a song. This revelation broke the confines around which normal Jazz soloing was based at that time. In simple terms it meant following the vertical, rather than horizontal, progression of a tune. Charlie found with this understanding he could start at any point in the scale and still resolve the dissonance in the phrase. From that moment Bird soared.

When he met the trumpeter Dizzy Gillespie, he found a kindred spirit and together laid the foundations for the evolution of a new form of Jazz: Bebop.

Bebop is characterised by complex improvisation and played at fast tempo. Many of the tunes played used the chords of standard tunes, but were played in such a radically different form that the artists avoided paying the original copyright, as in Parkers version of *How high the moon,* which he renamed *Ornithology.* It was acrobatic, it was revolutionary, the antithesis of the popular swing dance music of the time, too fast to dance to and demanding listening. The sentiment of the Beboppers was summed up by the Jazz pianist Thelonious Monk, who was quoted as saying, "we wanted a music that they couldn't play", "they" referring to the white swing band leaders.

Opinion about the quality of Bebop was split between extremes, some hailing it as genius, others as rubbish.

Beboppers called the traditionalist 'Mouldy figs' while the traditionalists called Bebop 'Chinese music', Louis Armstrong condemned it as "no melody to remember and no beat to dance to." Controversy raged on but Bebop spread, spawning a racially integrated following and subculture of admirers known as Hipsters. Dizzy and Bird toured together but their compatibility became more confined to music, as Bird's drug taking and heavy drinking made him unreliable. Often turning up late to gigs, or not at all, forcing Dizzy to take on an extra band member to cover for Bird's absences.

When Dizzy returned to New York, Bird stayed on in Los Angeles and signed up with Ross Russell on the Dial label, producing many of his most memorable recordings in this period, including an iconic take of Gillespie's *A night in Tunisia,* in which he performed a dazzling solo, which simply became known as "The famous Alto break". Unfortunately Bird's life seemed to be a series of peaks and troughs and only a few months later he had to be held up to the microphone while recording *Lover Man,* close to collapse, intoxicated on cheap whiskey that he'd used as a substitute for withdrawal from heroine. Bird was furious when Russell released the record, but although not technically perfect; the fragility of the performance gives an insight into his soul, and is one of my favourite Charlie Parker recordings.

Soon after the notorious *Lover Man* session Charlie had a nervous breakdown and was committed to the state mental hospital. After six months there he recovered and returned to

New York with his own quintet, including a young Miles Davis on trumpet. Bebop was at its height of popularity and Bird's stunning agility on the saxophone amazed audiences in the clubs on fifty-second street, the centre of the Bebop world. He was invited to the 1949 Paris Jazz festival and toured with great success, finding Europeans much more accommodating and liberal towards black artists than attitudes back home.

On his returned to the States he was reinvigorated and had a new project on his mind; fascinated by Stravinsky he decided to make a long playing record backed up with strings. It was an audacious scheme, classical music normally the preserve of white artists, and some fans of Bebop accused him of selling out. The record certainly broadened his popularity and its commercial success proved his respectability across cultures. A club on Broadway was named after him, Birdland, and people flocked to see him.

By the early 1950's Bird was at the height of his fame, living in New York with his partner at that time and their children. I saw him riding a white horse down Seventh Avenue; he's wearing a pinstriped suit, a yellow tie and a fedora. People on the street are waving and calling to him as he goes by, life is fine and he can do anything, even be a cowboy in New York. He acknowledges his fans and continues on to a tavern where he dismounts and ties the horse up outside. Inside other Jazz musicians greet him and admire his dashing entrance, there is much laughter and joshing of Charlie's jape, everyone wants to buy him a drink, Birds the man.

Somehow Charlie was managing to lead three fulltime lives: Bird the musician, Bird the family man and Bird the addict. It was taking its toll and his lifestyle was beginning to affect his health. When he was unable to score heroin he used alcohol to fill the void and was diagnosed with bleeding ulcers from his excessive drinking. At the same time the authorities were cracking down on the drug related Jazz scene after a number of musician deaths were blamed on drug overdoses. Charlie was arrested, and although released, his cabaret card was confiscated. Without it he was unable to work in New York, and he was forced to tour away from home. Eventually the ban was revoked, on the pleas of Charlie, so that he could work and pay the doctor's fees needed for the illness of his young daughter. Unfortunately the doctors were unable to help her and his daughter died.

Charlie's drug and alcohol problems became worse and his erratic behaviour led to him being fired from Birdland. He attempted suicide and a short spell in hospital followed, but his health and mental state had deteriorated beyond recovery. He'd hit rock bottom. I saw him return to Birdland, one night with a friend, but the door man won't let him in, says he dressed too casually and it doesn't matter who he is. The clubs neon light is flashing 'Birdland' and its namesake is standing forlornly looking up at the sign and then at his feet. He turns to his friend "Can you imagine that?" he says in disbelief. "They name a club after me and won't even let me in." He's no longer a bird, he's a broken man.

A year after his daughter's death Charlie Parker passed away in the apartment of a Jazz patron that he'd stayed at after being taken ill on the way to a performance. Aged thirty four, his body was in such poor condition the medical examiner estimated he was nearly twice that age. It is easy to focus on Birds hedonistic lifestyle and lose sight of his incredible musical talent and contribution to Jazz. His birthday is still celebrated by a saxophone salute at his graveside every year and his legacy inspired a whole new generation of players, including Miles Davis and John Coltrane. I turned the last page of the book, the final words were those of Miles Davis, succinctly summarising the history of Jazz, "Louise Armstrong; Charlie Parker." I closed the book and wondered why so many great musicians ended up dead before their time.

My fascination with Charlie Parker's music grew, it wasn't just his melodic improvisation but the way he accented his rhythmic interpretation. The flow of his music took all sorts of unexpected twists and turns, his creativity was genius. I was inspired and tried to practise more, but my bottom lip was sore. I looked in the mirror and noticed it was discoloured and swollen. Great! I looked like I'd been for a Botox treatment. Saxophone forums said this was normal, so I just had to suffer for my art.

I was out one day resting my lip, standing on the rocks on the seafront watching the surf. As I scanned the horizon the Witch paddled by in a surf kayak and cut down the front of a wave. She braced with her paddle and turned the boat at right angles to the break, achieving a pop out. As the kayak upended she managed to pirouette it and land the right way up facing out to sea. Lazily she paddled out beyond the surf, did an Eskimo roll and surfaced, giving me and casual wave, before disappearing out of sight around the edge of the rocks.

When she re-appeared she was on a surf board, in a day-glow spandex swimming costume. I wondered whether it was a bit cold for that sort of exposure in November, but she seemed undeterred. With the music to *Wipe out* playing she caught a wave as the creamy top curled over to form a barrel. The music changed to the Beach Boys *Surfing USA*, and although it sounded strangely incongruous in West Wales on a wintery afternoon, it seemed to encourage Eleanor to greater heights of daring and she rode the tube, looking rather spectacular. The wave died and she paddled over to my look out post.

"That was pretty good," I said admiring her technique.

"Thanks," she said with a shrug, "you just have to go with the ride, why don't you call by soon?"

"Okay," I said as she caught another wave to the chorus of *I Wish they could all could be Californian Girls,* and disappeared into the big Blue.

When I returned to Eleanor's garden Bird was there with his sax, Dizzy was on trumpet, Thelonious Monk on piano, Buddy Rich on drums and Curly Russell on bass, making up the typical formation of a Bebop band. They were all wearing berets and bop glasses, and were playing Birds song, *Ko-Ko*, inspired by his love of the Jazz classic *Cherokee*. Monk, once described by the poet, Philip Larkin, as "the elephant on the piano", was being quite restrained in his accompaniment, and gave me a cheeky grin as Diz and Bird exchanged licks.

Dizzy's pouched hamster cheeks bellowed in and out with his efforts, and despite its fast tempo he and Bird came together with perfect ease and synchronicity at the beginning and end of the tune, playing with dazzling virtuosity. The solos were outrageous and, as John Coltrane said when he first heard Bird play, "It smacked me right between the eyes". I felt the same way, the improvisation made me feel off balance, it had a pattern, but was hard to follow because it wasn't a pattern I was used to.

Eleanor was reclining on the lawn in a stripy deck chair, flamboyantly smoking a cigarette attached to long filter tip. I think she was trying to be hip, wearing a beret and Bebop glasses like the rest of the band, which was a better look than the Spandex I had last seen her in. The tune finished and Eleanor applauded loudly shouting "Bravo! Bravo!" and got up and draped herself over Thelonious's piano, "Darlings," she said rather theatrically, "that was marvellous." She sucked energetically on the end of her filter and exhaled a vast cloud of smoke which Thelonious disappeared behind with an explosive coughing fit. Eleanor ignored him and continued, "You simply must come again, don't you think Jess?"

"Definitely, thanks, it was great. How did you do that?" I asked Bird. I was feeling a bit star struck and was trying to think of something more eloquent to say, but was still in shock after listening to the Bebop sound. Fortunately Charlie took my remark as an intelligent question and gave me his measured response.

"I realised by using the high notes of the chords as a melodic line, and by the right harmonic progression, I could play what I heard inside me. That's when I was born."

Thelonious crashed a few chords agreeing with Charlie's answer, before vanishing with the rest of the band into the smog now engulfing most of the garden. Eleanor returned to her deck chair and flopped back into it, waving her cigarette around doing her best Ava Gardner impression. Concerned about the health effects of secondary smoking I decided to follow the band's lead and disappear, finding myself back running on the beach, the strains of *Ko Ko* still lingering in my mind.

Chapter 8. New Directions

We are not retreating - we are advancing in another direction. (Douglas MacArthur)

Now Jay and I met less frequently I mostly played music by myself, but once a month there was a session in the local pub and the chance for a more sociable musical exchange. It seemed to be an event of extremes, either very quiet or very noisy, and as soon as I arrived in the car park, one Saturday late in November, it was apparent it was going to be one of those noisy evenings.

I was greeted by a bunch of drunken Hooray Henrys standing by the entrance door. "I say are you English?" one young man said in a fruity voice. The group were dressed in Christmas jumpers and plus fours and easy to characterised as 'Tim, nice but dim' types. I didn't bother answering, not only because they appeared past the point of any intelligent conversation but also my attention had been diverted by Jay, Matt and Faantastic Bob, who were outside having a smoke. Jay had recently met up with Bob and invited him along to the evening. Bob was always up for some music, especially as the Muddy River Boys were presently disbanded, and it hadn't taken much persuasion for him to join us.

"Jess, give us a hug," Bob boomed in his West Country accent. I hugged him, it was lovely to see him, he hadn't changed a bit, and after a chat we squeezed past the Henry's and into the pub. It was just like old times with Bob making me laugh with his indignant recounting of the latest outrages he perceived had been committed by Vic, the Muddies band leader, and eulogising about the "faantastic" music he heard when he'd been out somewhere. He seemed to be enjoying the present evening's entertainment as much as his other musical adventures, enthusiastically joining in with the double bass and singing a few songs on guitar in his own inimitable fashion.

Bob's double bass had recently had a bit of a makeover after a nasty incident with a caravan door, which had necessitated some serious first aid from Bob, who had seemingly finished off his repairs by painting the body with black tar. It looked a bit odd, but sounded okay, unfortunately the Henry's seemed to think so too and joined us, one of them offering to play Bobs black beast. That didn't really work so they tried clapping out of rhythm instead and then singing, which was even worse as they just kept repeating the same unimaginative sentence which sounded something like "We are English." Actually it was hard to know they were saying, as too much alcohol had made their lips go floppy and fall over their teeth, rendering them incapable of any proper pronunciation. We tried to ignore them and thankfully eventually they took the hint and disappeared into the pool room.

Once the Henry's had gone the evening proceeded more pleasantly. We had arrived before the pub got too crowded and carved out an area in the front bar with plenty of space to play in. Later arrivals to the pub became packed into the front bar, including a group of portly gentleman in red jersey's, which when you are living in 'the land of song', usually means a male voice choir. I hoped the Henry's would stay in the pool room and not try singing again, luckily it looked like the front bar was too congested to squeeze any more people into it, should they be tempted to try.

With numbers now favouring the Welsh contingent in the pub we finished off the evening with Sosban Fach, an unlikely Welsh folk tune about a harassed housewife and a saucepan, adopted as a rousing anthem by the Llanelli Scarlet's rugby union club. When sang at a rugby match the Welsh words of *Sosban fach yn berwi ar y tan, Sosban fawr yn berwi ar y llawr,* sound rather more inspiring than their English translation of *A little saucepan is boiling on the fire, A big saucepan is boiling on the floor,* a sentiment probably unlikely to strike fear into the opposition. The music has an East European feel to it, and Jay and I liked to play each verse a bit faster, as if it were a Cossack dance. I thought we played it quite well, although I didn't think they'd heard us in the adjoining bar. As we started to pack our stuff away a low sound started to rumble in the background, gradually swelling to the more thunderous noise of two dozen men singing in perfect harmony while crammed into a small space. It felt like everything was vibrating, I didn't recognise the song, but the Welsh sentiment was unmistakeable.

"They're the best male voice choir in the area," a lady with a Welsh accent confided in me, "win all the competitions they do." I could certainly believe that and headed back home with a warm feeling of nostalgia inside me. The Witch sat silently in the passenger seat staring straight ahead dressed in the Welsh national costume, obviously overcome with nationalistic sentiment engendered by the evening's performance. I sensed that she was contemplating a rousing chorus of *Land of my Fathers,* "Don't even think about it," I warned her. Miffed, she remained silent for the rest of the journey and didn't reply when I drew up outside the house and bid her "Nos Da", before going into the house. I went to bed and lay in the dark thinking about the evening, which had been fun, but as the end of the year approached, it was time to start thinking about some new musical challenges and fresh horizons.

Much as I enjoyed the violin I was enjoying the sax more. Using your mouth to play an instrument felt more intimate and connected than using a bow and as beginner the rewards, in terms of progress, were much greater. Once I had grasped the basic technique of playing sax I found that although technically it was fundamentally different to the violin, in some ways it was similar, in that both instruments need the player to create the sound, rather than being able to immediately strike the right note, like on a piano or guitar. This makes them very expressive to play and I found I was able to use a lot of the musical knowledge I had gained from playing the violin in the last few years to help me play on the sax.

After I had been playing the sax for a couple of months, and it was nearing the end of the hire time, I knew I wanted to buy one and invest as much money and time as I could into it. I withdrew all my savings and contacted Windband, asking what Saxes they stocked in the maximum price range I could afford. There were two, a Japanese one and a Selmer, sax royalty, Charlie Parker's choice of sax to buy with his insurance money. The chance of owning a Selmer held a romantic notion for me, but I wanted to be objective about it and decided I would go and carry out a blind testing.

I caught the early train and with a deep breath and feeling of destiny entered the small room at the back of the Windband shop where the two Saxes were laid out. I picked up the one closest to me and kept my eyes adverted from any clues as to which it might be, however by the time I had attached the reed and ligature I thought I had spotted it was the Selmer. I picked it up and clipped it on to the neck strap and placed my hands on the buttons, it felt uncomfortable and completely different to the one I had been playing, maybe I just needed to get used to it. I blew into it and a disappointing note came out, there was no timbre to the tone and I felt disenchanted, I desperately wanted to fall in love with the Selmer and it wasn't happening.

I tried for half an hour to make it sound nice, and although it did eventually sound better it definitely wasn't a love match. I put it down and reluctantly picked up the other one. Despite my lack of enthusiasm it immediately felt right, there were little dimples on the buttons which helped my fingers sink into them and when I played it a soft smoky note came out. I cursed the Japanese; it was everything I wanted in a sax, except it had the wrong name. I told myself it shouldn't matter, it was the chosen one and I would have to suppress my dreamy ideas about playing a

Selmer. I played it for a while and it only got better. I unclipped it and looked more closely at it and laughed, it WAS the Selmer and we were meant to be together.

By the time I had sorted out the mouthpiece I had been in the shop nearly an hour and a half and there seemed to be a long queue of people waiting to try out instruments in the room I had been occupying. Well, they wouldn't be trying the Selmer, because they only kept one in stock, and I was walking out with it strapped to my back. I'd never spent so much on an instrument, or so well, and the thrill stayed with me, constantly making me want to pick it up and play.

...

Although I was finding it increasingly hard to drag myself away from the sax, a couple of small projects arose to spotlight a little bit of focus on my neglected violin. Firstly, while chatting on a sax forum I met a local DJ, Richie, who really enjoyed our Outlaw Jones CD and played a few tracks on his show and interviewed me about the music. I was not sure that there were too many people listening but it was nice to feel our music was appreciated and played over the airwaves. It was also that time of year when people produce a Christmas record and I decided to make an exclusive one for my mother, who was my number one fan and keen for more books and music. Well, the present book and sax were an ongoing progress, but I thought a live music session in the kitchen with Jay might suffice, and asked him whether he could help for a small fee.

Jay wasn't very keen, I think for all sorts of reasons; his mind was on other things, and he probably just wanted to move on from feeling any obligations towards me. Anyway he agreed, but there was only time for a couple of short sessions before the Christmas deadline. I arrived late one afternoon, after work, and plugged in my small hand recorder, placing it on the kitchen table. The kitchen was chosen as it was usually the only room in the house where Jay lit the fire, therefore making it warm enough for fingers to work, and also provided good acoustics with its slate floors and high ceiling.

I unpacked my four string violin, which I had just gone back to after playing the five string for the last two years. The change had arisen after taking another block of lessons with Sarah in the autumn, when I had played her four string and realised how much smaller and easier it was to handle than a five string. I had commissioned Jay to replace the pegs, bridge and strings, and it hadn't settled down yet, frequently going out of tune. I was still playing it in and getting used to it, and in retrospect it probably wasn't the most sensible thing to use, but when you're doing a live recording that's what happens. On top of a temperamental violin, another unanticipated event was Jimmi's appearance, tiptoeing around the kitchen making soup. The play back revealed the scrapping chairs and clinking spoon of our 'little' visitor, along with intermittent musical mistakes. Despite these glitches, I was reasonably pleased with the quality of the music, and Jay burnt off a few copies for me in time for Christmas.

It looked like any future recording wouldn't be interrupted by the appearance of Jimmi, who was in the process of moving into a small flat in the village not far from where I lived. In fact, as Jimmi said, as we stood admiring the sea views, we were practically neighbours. Jimmi wasn't good with change, it had taken him a long time to build up to this moment, but his differences with Jay, together with the instability of the house being on the market, and the cold dark shadows of the mountains of Dolwen, had pushed him into it. Having made the decision, moving was now proving to be a slow and protracted process, not helped by the position of his new residence at the top of a five story building. I said I would help him, but the first time had been thwarted by the lack of light as Jimmi battled with the electricity metre and we ended up sitting in the dark drinking some bottles of beer that I had found fortuitously in the van.

The next time I went there it was Jimmi's birthday. I had been to the local recycling plant to try and find some furniture for him to set up his recording gear and help him stop living off the floor. Jumping out of the van I spotted the perfect thing straight way, a solid music centre that could be stacked or broken down into three separate units, great for the low ceilings in Jimmi's flat, and giving him plenty of table top area for his computer and sound desk. It all fitted neatly into the van along with a bench, office chair and three garden chairs for his balcony. I arrived with the booty and Jimmi was chuffed, but wanted to shift the heavier units using the rope and pulley he had specially ordered to avoid carrying things up the stairs.

"But isn't it going to swing under the stair case here and get stuck?" I said doubtfully as we stood at the top of the fire escape and Jimmi attached the pulley to the railing.

"Well we can probably lean over and grab it from there," Jimmi said optimistically. Since Jimmi would be holding the rope I wasn't sure how "we" would achieve this without permanent damage to my back, but Jimmi was determined to defy gravity with engineering acumen. A bunch of Stone Age men, veterans of moving the huge blocks of stone into place at Stonehenge, had appeared on the balcony, appraising our labours. They were very muscular and hairy, dressed in animal skins and each of them carried a thick wooden club. There was lots of muttering between them and shaking of heads, appearing to indicate a certain lack of optimism about our furniture moving plan. The pulley attachment was somewhere down by our knees, which meant Jimmi had to start walking back down the fire escape to make it work. The builder's bag, containing one of the units, rose about five feet in the air before Jimmi had to admit defeat, and lowered it back down to accompanying jeers from our audience.

Jimmi refused to be beaten, "I'll double the rope and use my body weight to pull from below," was his next plan. After rethreading the rope he went down the steps and pulled from ground level as I watched him from the top. The Stone Age men, who by now I had decided were called Ugg, Nugg, Fump, and Wump, had also gone down and stood round in a semi-circle cheering him on. Once again the unit was lifted until it reached about five feet in the air and then stopped. "I need gloves,"

Jimmi called up, "or I'm going to get rope burn." The load slowly spiralled down again and there was a groan of disappointment from Ugg, Nugg, Fump, and Wump before they trudged off, clubs over their shoulders, disgruntled with our efforts. I coiled the rope up and we heaved the three units up by hand in about half the time we had spent messing about with the pulley. It was definitely worth the hard work and I left Jimmi happily sorting through his boxes and leads and setting up his recording gear.

Although the music unit had been a success, Jimmi still didn't have anywhere comfortable to sit. I returned to the recycling plant a few days later, a suit of furniture on my wish list, one that, that could easily be got up the fire escape without being jeered at by a bunch of Stone age men. I was determined to prove that evolution had worked and I could outsmart an ancient forebear when it came to moving bulky items around. It was late afternoon, getting dark and drizzling, but I spotted the ideal thing as soon as I drove into the yard, the Witch was sitting on the two seat sofa, waving to me, with two matching chairs and table in front of her. A wicker furniture conservatory set, solid and in good condition, that even I could easily lift without help.

Half an hour later I was still at the recycling plant, with the recycling man, trying to solve the conundrum of how to get the five pieces of furniture to fit it into the van. We had tried various combinations of sofa in first, sofa in last, table in the front, table in the back, chairs on top of table, chairs underneath the table, but there was always one piece of furniture left out. It was like some giant puzzle, which had me and the recycling man both scratching our heads. Ugg, Nugg, Fump, and Wump had appeared, but had quickly got bored and were leaping about the yard smashing things up with their clubs. The Witch had also lost interest and appeared to have fallen asleep in the chair that wouldn't fit into the van. It looked like it was going to have to be left behind, but as soon as I had thought that, the Witch opened one eye and pointed behind her, a lady was getting out of a car and I realised I knew her.

"Hi Caitlin, I don't suppose you're going back my way and if so can fit this chair in your car?" I asked hopefully.

"Sure, no problem," she said happily and the problem was solved. I drove out of the yard and waved to the Witch, who responded in kind. Ugg, Nugg, Fump, and Wump didn't notice me go, they were busy in the plastic recycling skip, using it as a kind of bouncy castle and clubbing each other over the head as they jumped up and down. I was glad they were having a good time, even if I was unable to share with them my tips for moving awkward objects around the countryside in the modern era.

Jimmi was delighted with his furniture. He was able to pimp it up with rugs and throws, and move it around whenever the mood took him. He still wasn't reconciled to letting go of his dream of returning to Shady Grove and being involved in a permaculture lifestyle, but I hoped his pain would ease as he became more settled in at the flat. His mate Mo arrived and helped him bring a load of stuff back from Dolwen, and carry up the twenty five kilo box of rice that Jimmi had been carrying around in the car for the last week. Jimmi worried about the stability of the economy and like to safeguard against future uncertainties, now finally he seemed to have found himself a home which he could fill with his stockpiles of staples, as well as herbs, spices and Himalayan salt.

Jimmi was very enthusiastic about the benefits of Himalayan salt, both for internal and external use, and emitting negative ions into the atmosphere to restore air quality. He had bought large quantity of it, in its raw form, his flat was littered with chiselled pink rocks, some so big that they needed two hands to lift. When needed, for cooking or washing, he would chip lumps off and grind them up. Normal salt was just refined sodium chloride, Jimmi explained, but Himalayan salt had all the essential minerals our body needed and offered to give me some of his precious supplies. I was a bit reticent about trying to hack pieces off a boulder at the dinner table. I was glad when he dragged out a large sack of crystals and dipped a jar into it, handing me the full container. It certainly tasted good and I happily took his gift home with me, soon becoming a convert to its taste and health benefits.

For the moment things seemed on the up for Jimmi, and as he lived close to where I shopped, ran, and wrote in my van, I seemed to be seeing quite a lot of him. Obliging with tea and comfort, I increasingly enjoyed his company and I called by on Christmas morning, taking my Selmer, for him to admire. He was duly impressed and I played some carols, making him laugh. We had a quick jam together, playing one of the first tunes I had learnt to play, *Isn't she lovely"* by Stevie Wonder, before I left to regale Seb and Jules with more tunes and spend the rest of the day with them.

With Christmas done I looked ahead to the New Year, hoping I could find someone to play music with on a regular basis. I decided to ask Eleanor about it as I stormed up Cadair Idris one snowy morning. It was absolutely freezing and the only way I could stay warm was to walk very fast up the buttress that led on to the summit ridge. Eleanor appeared on a set of skis on the sky line and started a dashing descent towards me, somehow carving perfect parallel turns over the lumpy white ground. Behind her, Ugg, Nugg, Fump and Wump were clinging onto a sledge which was also hurtling down at great speed. They were totally out of control, hitting various tussocks and rocks with accompanying yells, but somehow they managed to hang on until a large boulder did for them, and they all flew through the air and landed in a heap in a snow drift, their legs waving in the air. Eleanor gracefully came to a stop beside me, showering me with snow.

"Thanks," I said shaking off the freezing crystals, "just when I was starting to warm up."

"Oh don't worry about that, let's go somewhere a bit hotter", Eleanor dismissed my complaint and the next moment we were on a beach on a tropical island. I was still in my ski gear, but Eleanor had changed into floral beach dress, Charlie Parker was there in a Hawaiian shirt and the Stone Age men were in their ubiquitous animal skins, although there were wearing spotted ones, which I assumed was their summer attire.

"What are they doing here?" I asked rolling my eyes.

"Well you said you needed someone to play with," said Eleanor with a shrug, "and they make a great backup band."

In saying so Ugg, Nugg, Fump and Wump each picked up a pair of brightly painted maracas laid out on the beach.

"We could call them the Rolling Stones," said Eleanor brightly,

"I think that's been done," I said dryly, "how about the Clubbing Lunatics?" I suggested as Fump and Wump started to bash each other over the head with their Maracas.

"Excellent idea!" said Eleanor, "boys let's begin."

The Clubbing Lunatics came to order and started shaking their Maracas while Eleanor tapped out a Latin Jazz rhythm on some bongos and Bird started to play *My Little Suede Shoes* on his sax, one of his bestselling tunes. The "boys" were doing a little dance routine to it, which occasionally involved hitting each other, but on the whole they were reasonably behaved and the music swung quite well.

"Very good," I clapped at the end. "Wish I could play like that," I said to Bird.

"Music is your own experience, your own thoughts, your wisdom. If you don't live it, it won't come out your horn," he said, in the slow thoughtful way he had of speaking.

"Absolutely," said Eleanor.

As I stood there absorbing Bird's insight a coconut flew by head and I was forced to duck. All-out war had ensued between the Clubbing Lunatics, with a ready supply of missiles lying around on the beach, we were all forced to run and take cover.

"I'll sort some people out for you to practise with, don't worry," Eleanor shouted from behind the palm tree where she had taken refuge, "but you'll need to explore some possibilities yourself, maybe some that you haven't even thought about. Have fun."

"Ok!" I yelled back behind my palm tree, deciding it was time to return to the safety of Cadair Idris. The mountains didn't seem quite so cold after my brief holiday to warmer climes and I noticed that as I carried on climbing towards the summit I left behind sandy footprints in the snow.

…

I had a vague memory of a patient I'd seen some years before who had been telling me about how she was learning to play the sax and that she had been playing with someone she'd met locally. I could picture the patient in my mind but couldn't remember her name, so I thought about her really hard and within a few days bumped into her. She gave me the name of the lady who worked in a local book shop so I went down there.

"Hi," I said to an assistant, "is there a lady called Mary who works here and plays the saxophone?"

Next moment I was chatting with a lively lady and exchanging email addresses. She was busy up to Christmas but once that had passed we arranged a meet at my house and she turned up one wet and windy night with her baritone sax. She also played tenor and soprano but thought as the baritone was an E flat sax it would be easier to play with me, having the same fingerings as the alto, just an octave lower. The baritone was much bigger and louder than I expected and I wondered what my neighbours were thinking. They had originally said they were quite happy for me to play sax, but when they had said "Go for it!" I guess neither they, nor I, had envisaged the monster which was now in my room, threatening to blow me through the adjoining wall and into their kitchen.

In its case I could barely pick it off the floor and Mary, who was a fine strong lady, had a special leather harness to hang it from around her neck, which looked like something a carthorse might wear. Mary was obviously blessed with a large pair of lungs and I could feel a blast of air coming out from the horn as she played and I thought that maybe it wasn't such a great idea to stand in front of it. The whole house, and my head, seemed to be vibrating with its resonance and I found it quite overwhelming compared to the soft sound of my Alto.

Mary played with great gusto, her style reflecting her personality. I soon renamed her 'Mad Mary' when she told me she occasionally hung several Saxes from her harness so she could easily switch from one to another. She liked to play in rock and roll bands where she used the baritone to provide the bass line or harmony, sometimes leaping into air while she played it. I'm not quite sure where this fitted in with my idea of playing Jazz, but played resolutely on in the gale being whipped up in the lounge, gripping tightly on to my Selmer and wondering whether Mary's enthusiasm would start to wane before the walls started to crumble and we were left standing in a pile of rubble.

Fortunately the house stood firm and we agreed to meet the following week, and Mad Mary wasn't the only one I was practising with. When Jay had found out that I was playing sax he didn't seem that impressed, but after we'd played together, admitted that it was more fun than he expected. It helped that he liked playing the Blues, which the sax leant itself to. The first Blues we played together was in E flat, not ideal on the guitar but the easiest fingerings for me. Jay played a basic twelve bar Blue chord sequence which I improvised over the top.

"Hmmm sounds kind of Egyptian," said Jay and Eleanor looked up from where she was knitting a scarf in front of the fire. I hadn't told him about the Witch and I wondered whether she was casting a spell on the music we were playing. We played the same tune again and Eleanor gave me a wink and got up and started doing her version of Wilson and Kepples sand dance, making me lose my concentration. I closed my eyes and tried to ignore her, but the seed had been planted and every time we played it afterwards the Witch did her dance.

Jay seemed increasingly distant when we played and I wondered how much longer we would continue to meet. In the future it looked like we might have to find somewhere else to rendezvous, as Jay had finally accepted an offer on the house. He was expecting the deal to go through soon, planning what he might do with the small amount of money left, after paying off the mortgage. His current dream was to go to Portugal in a lorry. It sounded a bit crazy, but I hoped he'd make it, last time he'd been thinking about such a trip he crashed his van and met me instead.

My timeline of events with Jimmi and Jay seemed to be going in reverse, and having spent the previous year helping Jay furnish and move into Dolwen, every time I visited I was now taking a load of Jimmi's stuff back with me, helping him move out. In gratitude Jimmi had invited me round to his flat one evening, for a curry, and I'd taken my sax, hoping to find him obliging to have a jam. He had seemed quite keen but I never knew with Jimmi, because he liked to say things to keep people happy without always meaning it. As it turned out it was an enjoyable session. We did some Blues with a backing track and took turns playing lead, Jimmi on his electric guitar, and me trying to imitate his phrasing my on sax.

I'd now been playing for three months and was surprised how comfortable I felt improvising and how quickly my sound had developed. Jimmi seemed to enjoy himself too and preferred playing with the sax rather than the violin, "Think you're a horny player rather than a stringy one," he said, with an embarrassed chuckle, after realising the innuendo. He suggested we have another play soon and as it was my birthday the following week he invited me around to celebrate.

I requested another curry, one of my favourite meals; Jimmi was a talented cook mixing ingredients the way he mixed records, ending up with delightful results in both cases. Afterwards we played the track we'd done the previous week, and recorded it first take. We were going to have a second run at it, but I was having problems with my reed, and when we listened to the playback I was surprised how good it sounded. It helped that Jimmi was such a clever sound recordist, who instinctively knew how to capture the sound and emphasise the right moments. After he twiddled a few nobs it took very little time before it was up on SoundCloud. Jimmi was chuffed and so was I, Jimmi liked no fussing, play, record, upload, job done in half an hour. I was pleased because if I kept practising I was only going to get better, especially if I could sort my reed out.

Woodwind players constantly fret about their reeds, because they are so crucial to the sound, and can spend hours debating brands, thickness and flexibility. You can get plastic ones, which are consistent and long lasting, but don't vibrate like a natural reed, or sound as good. The down side of natural reeds is that although they are machine cut, they are still variable in quality, take time to break in, need to be of certain moisture to work well, and invariably seem to break just as you are starting to like them. As a beginner I was finding it hard to judge where the problem lay. I'd just gone up a thickness, to give the higher notes better support, but it seemed really stiff to play. I decided to visit Terry again to ask his advice.

"It's either you, the sax or the reed," Terry concluded. Having established it wasn't my sax Terry went on to try the reed, "God it's like digging the garden," he spluttered after trying one, "terrible!" Eleanor tutted and shook her head in disgust from her position perched on top of the piano. Ugg, Nugg, Fump and Wump, were jumping up and down outside, trying to see through the window, they were too disruptive to be allowed in. We tried out the other two reeds I'd brought of the new strength, they were individually packaged and a top brand, but also duds. Terry gave me some advice on different reeds to try, gave me an exercise for double tonguing and starting the altissimo range.

That was the good thing about Terry; he gave me the information I asked for, without judging me, and he had a wealth of out printed books with little nuggets of information in that he could always lay his hands on. Armed with his information I left, phoned up the Windband and ordered a selection of reeds and a new leather ligature to secure them, having bent the delicate metal one I was using. They weren't going to arrive for a few days so taking my old reeds I went to the monthly pub session with Ally and drew my sax out for the first time. Matt was impressed and Bob said it was "faantastic", so it must have been alright.

On the way back Ally was chatting about familiar souls, "You, Jay and Jimmi have definitely all met in a previous life" she remarked. "Yes, definitely," I agreed. They were like family to me and I supposed it was why I felt so comfortable around Jimmi, and why I had started to let his hugs go on for longer than they should. I met him the following day in the steam room at the local leisure centre and sat down in the hot cloud, along with two other women he was already chatting to. Everyone seemed very happy considering they were being par boiled, and I wondered why it was that Jimmi got on so well with women whatever the circumstances.

We went back to Jimmi's and had some food and after which he asked if I wanted to record another track. "Yes, great. I just want to see how I'm sounding really. What about *Summertime*?" Jimmi searched for a suitable backing track and looped it so we could just keep playing. It had a smooth Jazz feel and we played for about ten minutes, swapping leads, before we drew it to a close. We listened to the play back.

"Pretty good," said Jimmi, "I'll just cut the first two minutes off when we were warming up." He clicked some buttons and listened again. "Think it needs a shaker," he said and disappeared into the kitchen, ignoring Ugg, Nugg, Wump and Fump who were jumping up and down with their maracas making "me, me, me" type noises, I guess he couldn't see them. He returned with a pot of basmati rice and shook it for a while into a speaker before putting the results onto the track. "There we go," said Jimmi, "percussion by the Rice Brothers, Baz n' Mati." The Clubbing Lunatics looked disappointed and sat pouting in a corner. Jimmi played back the finished track with an approving smile and put it up on SoundCloud along with Blues 28. When I listened to them I was surprised at the quality of the sound and the evident musical connection between us. As I responded to his riffs, he drew out an expression in me beyond the short time I had spent playing sax. Even when I hear these recordings now, this affinity strikes me every time.

He then spent a couple of hours sorting out my computer, which was full of virus's, cleaning it up and putting on firewalls for me, and a program that you could use to make interesting effects on photos, helping me change my profile picture on SoundCloud and Facebook. He was very clever with technology and finally sorted out the problem I had with Windows media player, which had imported all the viruses onto my computer in the first place.

"Anyway," he said sounding a bit hurt as he finished up, "I don't know why you say we've got nothing in common, we like the same food, playing music together, walks on the beach, taking photos and a bunch of stuff."

What he said was true, I thought, as I reciprocated his long hug, reflecting back on the day's events he was referring to and our walk earlier along the beach. Jimmi always took his camera on walks, taking pictures from unusual and interesting perspectives, capturing the world in beautiful moments, which showed a more sensitive man that belied his seemingly brash exterior. He said he wasn't like other people, and he wasn't, but that was one of the reasons I liked him. His interests varied from quantum mechanics to aliens, and although his views were often very different to my own, he made me think about paradigms I hadn't considered before.

I continued to help him with his move, lending a hand to bring back his precious memory foam mattress that had been left in his poly tunnel at Shady Grove. Crisis point had been reached after he had managed to burst the second air bed, since moving into his new flat, and was now sleeping on the floor. We were going up in two vehicles to bring back some more of his furniture, but of course nothing was ever that straight forward and as I passed Jimmi in a layby waving at me, I realised he had broken down. The spring had broken underneath the wheel arch and was ripping the wall of the tyre off as he drove.

Fortunately we were just outside the village and Jimmi slowly drove it back to where he could park it, until he could figure out how to get it repaired, and we continued on our way in my van. The rest of the trip involved a great deal of huffing and puffing as we bent the mattress into the van and dragged it up the five flights of steps into Jimmi's flat. Once the cover was washed, which along with the dirt of two years from being stored in a poly tunnel had now been added mud stains from being dragged across a field; Jimmi finally had something comfortable to sleep on.

Soon after our trip to Shady Grove I met him again at the sauna, along with Daz, a Scouse mate of Jimmi's, who had come to do some recording with him. Daz was starring forlornly at his feet, wondering why they looked like a pair of Weetabix, and decided to go and have a cold shower to try and find his toes. Jimmi looked across at me, the temperature was rising and droplets of water slowly trickled down the walls and dripped off the ceiling, soaking into the tight curls on his broad chest. The Witch gave me a hard stare through the steamy atmosphere and arched a knowing eyebrow.

Chapter 9. George

To withdraw myself from myself has ever been my sole, my entire, my sincere motive in scribbling at all. (Byron)

Daz went back to Liverpool the next day, arranging to meet Jimmi in London the following week to do some recording at a friend's studio. The interval passed quickly, and by the time Jimmi caught the train to London, I'd gone to work thinking some distance between us might be a good thing. I'd known Jimmi for several years, through all sorts of turmoil, and suddenly had all sorts of feelings for him that I didn't want, didn't make any sense, and I didn't feel were reciprocated in terms of any commitment towards me.

The Witch wasn't helping matters by spinning around in one of the office work chairs giving me "I told you so" looks on every rotation and I arrived back home feeling tearful and confused. I got a text from Jimmi asking if I was alright and when I replied, "Not really", he called. Hearing his warm Scouse voice over the phone made me feel better; perhaps I could act a bit more logically on his return. From his calls and texts I gathered that he was pretty bushed by the whole London experience, dragging his heavy steel guitar around on public transport and staying in some grotty hotel. "I had to get some bottled water, cause there are tentacles coming out the tap" he said morosely, which made me laugh, his weird take on life was one of the things about Jimmi that I related to.

"I'll pick you up from the station, and you can come round here for a meal if you like before I take you back to yours," I offered. I would be on home turf and it seemed like a safe environment to operate in, even though that afternoon I could feel a growing sense of anticipation as Jimmi hurtled towards me at 125 miles an hour on his Virgin express train. I'd made a fire and cooked some food, and Jimmi gratefully collapsed on the settee while I made a fuss over him reminding myself to keep my distance. Perhaps I should have reminded myself more.

"Well that went really well," said Eleanor with an edge of sarcasm after I had finally dropped Jimmi home, "nothing I admire more than a woman of resolve." Of course she was right and I realised it was probably better if I didn't see him for a while. I messaged him on Facebook and then went off to work to work the following morning wondering which one of us would crack first.

A series of angry texts popped up from Jimmi, who seemed to think we could carry on as we were and accusing me of all sorts of inconsistences, dragging up my marriage and past relationship with Jay, saying the present situation was my karma. He finished with a parting shot that I should sell my sax and take up golf. I didn't bother replying, there seemed no point in saying I didn't even like golf. I stared at the huge pile of patient discharges built into a wobbly tower in front of me, waiting for my attention. I glazed over and found myself in the Witches garden where there was a fight going on.

Ugg, Nugg, Wump and Fump were being chased around the lawn by a flamboyant young man brandishing a sword. He had a fine handsome face and his black curly hair flopped over the collar of the rather flouncy white shirt he wore. With his frilled cuffs, waistcoat, tight breaches and leather boots, his appearance suggested he was someone from the age of the Romantics and I noticed he had a slight limp as he ran about.

"He's still practising for the Greek war of independence," Eleanor shook her head; "he never got over it you know."

"Is that 'mad, bad and dangerous to know' Lord Byron?" I asked her.

"Yes dear, but you can call him George," she answered as we watched the chaos unfold in front of us. The Clubbing Lunatics had decided to take cover and they all leapt over the wall. When their heads popped up again they were each armed with some old wind fallen apples which they threw at George's head. Somehow George managed to impale them all on the end of his sword, like a giant fruit kebab, and then with a flick of his wrist he launched them back again, so that each Lunatic up with a squashed apple on the end of their nose. With a howl they all took off up the hill and George vaulted over the wall with a "Tally Ho" and raced after them.

"Anyway," I said, reflecting on George's warring ambitions, as I watched the five silhouettes appear as a distant line of running figures on the distant skyline, "Greece's situation hasn't changed much. It's just a slave to the International Monetary Fund now, rather than the Ottoman Empire. Same guys, different title. Not sure a sword is going to cut it nowadays. If George still wants Greek independence he should take on the banks. Was there any particular reason for his visit here today other than practising his fighting skills on four helpless Stone Age men?"

"Perhaps all those melancholic thoughts running around your head have invoked the spirit of *Manfred* and drawn him here?" Eleanor suggested.

"I hardly think my present angst compares to the tortured poetry of *Manfred*."

"Such a beautiful poem," she sighed; I was George's inspiration for the Witch of the Alps you know."

"Well you've changed your form a bit."

"I can change my form to anything I like," she sniffed, "and while I was about it I also rustled up the seven spirits for him."

"So, how come you managed to conjure up seven spirits for him whereas I get four Stone Age nutters?"

"Horses for courses dear and Byronic heroes are high maintenance. Anyway, why are you so glum?"

"Oh I don't know, I have feelings for Jimmi, but we have very different ideas about relationships. Now he's just dragged up a load of stuff from the past about my marriage, Jay, and made me feel bad."

My injuries came down on those who loved me
On those who I best loved: I never quell'd
An enemy, save in my just defence
But my embrace was fatal

I quoted from *Manfred*. Eleanor rolled her eyes at my desolate choice.

"Look people have choices, just as you do now. Be realistic about Jimmi and decide if that's what you want, as for the rest, learn from your mistakes and move on, and hope they do too.

Grief should be the instructor of the wise;
Sorrow is knowledge: they who know the most
Must mourn the deepest o'er the fatal truth

she quoted back at me. "You're not doing a *Manfred* are you and seeking forgetfulness?" she asked, looking a bit startled.

"No, I don't need spells, just a sounding board."

"Well that's a relief, poor Manfred spent far too much energy on seeking oblivion and not enough time dealing with his issues."

"Well, he was 'dealing' with it, in a sense; it was George's confessional wasn't it?"

"Yes dear, well you'd know all about that, anyway enough of this introspection, time for some music I think."

I turned around and Bird was there and he gave me a smile and started to play his signature tune *Now's the time.* Now was the time indeed and I was back in the Physiotherapy department under a pile of discharges.

I sent Jimmi a text and felt strong, I would tough it out. The next evening Crazy invited me over to see a film at the local cinema, *Into the Woods*. It had a witch in it so I thought I better go. "What do you think?" I whispered to Eleanor as Meryl Streep did her witchy thing.

"It's a bit old school dear, just look at the state of her finger nails, and when did she last use a moisturiser?" I had to agree Meryl was not looking at her best, although she did get a bit of a make-over at the end, which improved things. Afterwards Jules and Seb went straight home but I decided to stay on and watch the open mic, chiefly to see my next door neighbour performing. He had helped me solve a problem on my computer that morning, when the screen had suddenly decided to flip upside down, and I had realised after five minutes it was impractical to try and use it standing on my head. My clever neighbour had found the cunningly hidden flip button and righted the world.

As I sat listening to song after song about failed love at the open mic, I cracked and texted Jimmi, asking if he'd like to come for a drink, but he was already settled in for the night and didn't want move. By the time my neighbour had finished singing *You can't always get what you want, but if you try sometime you find you get what you need,* I decided it was time to leave, I could only take so much. When I got up the following morning I felt philosophical; relationships take time. I sent Jimmi a text, asking what time we'd meet at the pool, as we'd talked about. Jimmi reply seem to come from a completely different man to the one I'd made the arrangement with, I stared at it and read between the lines feeling a fool. I turned my phone off and went to the leisure centre by myself.

As I swum up and down the pool I speculated what the other disembodied heads might be thinking, and whether it was anything like what was going on inside mine. There was no sign of Eleanor or the boys, I was alone, and I found I couldn't swim away from my thoughts or sweat them out in the sauna either. I went home to watch Six Nations rugby, I hadn't looked at my phone as I didn't want to pick up messages from Jimmi, but unfortunately came across them as I went through my emails. Jimmi had invited me over the following day to finish some recording, and feeling it would be trite to refuse, I accepted. Before that I had to pay further penance, and go for a Valentines meal with Jules, Seb and their friends Mark and Jill.

There is nothing quite like having to work your way through several courses of food, feeling like you might vomit, or break down in tears, at any moment, while surrounded by loved up couples and the beautiful flowers that Seb had bought Jules. Seb had gone to a great deal of trouble making a curry but it was probably the last thing on earth I felt like eating. The Clubbing Lunatics stood by the table despondent and silent, until Ugg stepped forward and shyly presented me a single red rose. It was a touching thought, but didn't really help my composure and I made my excuses and escaped as soon as was decently possible.

Sunday morning dawned fair and I decided I needed to go sailing. I hadn't been since the summer and suddenly the thought of being out on the water and leaving my troubles on the shore, for a while, was appealing. Conditions were ideal and my

Laser sped over the water smoothly, the side tilted up with the pressure of the wind in the sail, until I leant back and used my weight to balance the boat. George appeared and sat alongside, the wind blowing back the curls from his face, as he braced the boat with me. He had a long thick woollen coat on, and laughed as his cheeks were splashed by the salty water, answering the wave with some prose.

There is pleasure in the pathless woods, there is rapture in the lonely shore,
There is society where none intrude, by the deep sea and music in its roar;
I love not Man the less, but Nature more.

"Ain't that the truth," I said and let the sail out, so the boat drifted on the tide, and I could dig out my mobile phone from my dry-suit and take some pictures.

"What are you doing and what is that?" he asked intrigued.

"It's called a phone and I'm taking some pictures with it." He looked at me blankly. "Don't they give you give you any updates where you come from?" His expression didn't change. "I'll take that as a no then. Look." I showed him the video on my phone and he appeared impressed.

"Remarkable. What are you going to do with the video?"

"Put it up on Facebook I think; it's kind of like publishing," I said hurriedly before George got too confused. Do you want to put some prose to it?

"Hmm," he frowned, "how about, *I only go out to get me a fresh appetite for being alone,* that's why you're here isn't it?"

"Yes" I said as I looked into the distance and wondered why Jimmi, of all men, should intrude, upon my splendid isolation.

"Would you like me to come with you to Jimmi's later?" he asked kindly.

I was circumspect, this was the original nineteenth century 'bad boy' whose scandalous love life had resulted in his self-imposed exile, and whose notoriety often took precedence over his poetry. Although, he was well schooled in affairs of the heart, so maybe he was my ideal champion. "Yes, thanks," I said and smiled gratefully at him.

"Take courage lady, *the heart will break, but broken live on.*"

"I know", I said, "just needs a bit a sticky tape and it will be fine." George looked at me quizzically, but both of us were suddenly distracted by the commotion of Eleanor and the Clubbing Lunatics hurtling by on a skiff. Eleanor, Fump and Wump were all on the wire while Ugg and Nugg clung to the mast terrified. They had right to be because the estuary was not a good place to sail such a boat and the next moment they had pranged into a sand bank and come to an abrupt halt. Ugg and Nugg were catapulted screaming into the water, while the others flew forward on their trapeze wires. Eleanor managed to round the bow of the boat, on hers, before they all flew back the other way and landed in the out-rigging with a groan. After a great deal of splashing and shouting Ugg and Nugg eventually hauled themselves back on deck. George and I looked at each other, decided that no words were needed, and I pulled in the main sheet and headed back to shore.

I had been thinking what I was going to say to Jimmi, but after I played the various options through my head decided they were all a waste of time. I dragged myself up the five flights of stairs and met him at the door with a cursory nod and went through into the bedsit and set up my sax. Shielding myself with a cold disembodied feeling I went through the motions of playing to the backing track of *Sunny* that we had been working on. Jimmi tried to give me a hug but I think my folded arms and stiff body soon gave him the message, and George pricked him with his sword a few times for good measure.

"Don't look so sad it might never happen," Jimmi said seemingly confused by my persona.

"It already has," I said tersely and left as soon as I could and went home.

Jimmi sent me the finished version on SoundCloud and technically it might have been better than the other two tracks we'd done, but I took no pleasure in it.

"You must eat" said George looking concerned as I sat there vacantly. Unfortunately, the fridge was full of curry and as I forced some down, passed the lump in my throat, I wondered if I'd ever be able to eat curry again without feeling sick. I went to bed but after a few hours' sleep I was disturbed by George who was shaking me, insisting I got up and wrote to Jimmi. "Why bother?" I asked crossly.

"But words are things, and a small drop of ink, falling like dew, upon a thought, produces that which make thousands, perhaps millions think," George returned eloquently.

"Okay," I grumbled and got out of bed, "you can help write it, but it better be twenty first century speak and I'm sending an email, no ink."

I got the lap top out and typed, with George constantly interrupting and adding his suggestions.

"Don't you think it's a bit cutting?" I asked hesitantly after reading back over it.

"Let him decide on the truth of it," George advised.

I wondered about the wisdom of this, given that among George's many witty excesses he had referred to the British foreign secretary, Viscount Castlereagh, as an "intellectual eunuch," William Wordsworth as "Turdsworth", had noted that the Portuguese had few vices "except lice and sodomy", and mercilessly put down the Keswick poets cliché of Wordsworth, Coleridge and Southey, in his poem Don Juan, suggesting they swap their Lakes for an ocean. George's strong point was definitely not subtly and his outrageous remarks not for the faint hearted.

I pressed the send button, feeling like I was launching a nuclear weapon, and then got up and went to work. After I finished I went round to visit Jay to drop off a few treats for his birthday and see how he was getting on. When I arrived he was on the phone and I got out my mobile and picked up my emails while he talked. An outburst of invective appeared from Jimmi. I had been expecting it but it was still shocking. By the time Jay finished his call I was reeling, but tried to pretend everything was normal; genuinely thrilled that Jay was exchanging contracts on his house the following day.

We played a few tunes before Jay had to get ready to go out. Unfortunately the last tune Jay decided to play was the Blues, *Sky is Crying,* which threw me completely off balance and tears came into my eyes and I had to play my violin with my back to him, and then I left. Jay didn't ask what was wrong and I didn't offer, the only man left in my life was George.

I finally got home after driving over the mountain road, continuously playing *Loverman* (Oh where can you be), on the CD player and nearly hitting several walls. It was a version recorded by the Charlie Watts quintet. The Rolling Stones drummer had nurtured a long standing dream to play Jazz, and as a young man he had written and illustrated a children's book about his hero, Bird. His success with the Stones had finally allowed him to pursue his passion and in the nineties he'd formed a quintet to record an album to accompany the republishing of his book, 'Ode to a High Flying Bird'. My fascination with Bird led me to track a copy of the CD down through the miracle of EBay. It was the first time I'd heard a version of Loverman sung and the singer had a very melancholic voice, like a sax, dragging every nuance of emotion from the words. I arrived home feeling suitably tortured.

I opened my front door to find haunting fragrance of curry lingering in the air, my son had discovered the vat of it in the fridge and cooked up a storm before he'd gone out. I lit an incense stick, trying to banish the smell, and sought something more appetizing to eat, finally settling on some quiche, which I burnt in the oven as I read more inflamed emails from Jimmi. I had deeply wounded his ego and he hit back as hard as he could, only his comment that I was "about as much fun to play with as a traffic warden", gave me a moment of light relief.

At one o'clock in the morning, after being battered by Jimmi's seventh email, I decided to reply, and asked him not to contact me unless he could be more civil. Everything felt wretched. "The great art of life is sensation, to feel we exist, even in pain," said George philosophically, but his words brought me no comfort as I finally fell into an exhausted sleep. The following morning it was difficult to concentrate on anything, I tried some music and George even came for a run with me, but nothing eased the dull ache I felt inside. Later on in the afternoon I ended up on the seafront reading George's epic satiric poem, Don Juan, his acerbic wit and observations on the hapless love life of the hero, making me laugh out loud.

"George you're so funny, only you could turn the classic legend of a womaniser on its head, as someone who is actually seduced by women."

"Story of my life." said George innocently.

"Yeah right, that's what Jimmi says too," I said cynically.

Right on cue a message pinged up on my mobile from Jimmi, telling me I could "Kiss his butt", but with a smiley, from which I adjudged he had calmed down. I invited him around for a coffee in the van while George went for a walk. Jimmi appeared a little while later, nearly knocking himself out as he smashed his head trying to insert himself through the vans sliding door, not realising it was actually Ugg sitting on the van roof, who had hit him over the head with his club, delivering his own verdict on the situation. While it might not have been Uggs intension, the effect of his blow immediately dispelled the tension between us, as Jimmi sat down dizzily and I anxiously checked for the effects of concussion. Soon we were sitting together, and as we watched the sun set we talked, agreeing that there only was the present, which was a present, and for the moment nothing else mattered.

...

The troubled waters between myself and Jimmi continued to bubble, but meanwhile other sagas were finally drawing to a close with Jay finally completing the sale of the house at Dolwen. Jimmi and I went over one last time to collect anything that might come in useful. As the three of us stood together for one last time, amongst all the dismantled debris scattered about the floors, I wondered what the significance was of what we had built there; where the hopes and dreams had gone, was there anything left of that time, and had it been worth it. At least Jay had emerged from the episode with some money, ambition, and new love. I had offered to help him move, but he declined, he was now independent and free and had a new sense of determination about him.

The echoes of the half empty house made me feel gloomy and I couldn't wait to leave. I jumped into Jimmi's car, squeezing a last towel and picture in the back, most of the space was already taken up with a fridge/freezer which had been festering in one of the outhouses. The interior of the fridge looked like it had been used for brewing a deadly culture, suitable for the most advanced form of germ warfare. After we dragged it up the stairs, onto Jimmi's balcony we blasted it with bleach, eventually discovering a white interior underneath all the grey mould and bacteria. The seals didn't fit properly around the doors, but Jimmi brilliantly solved the problem by greasing them all with Vaseline, thereby creating such powerful suction effect I could barely open the doors at all.

The whole cleaning process might have been emblematic of something, but I couldn't think what and I arrived home slightly depressed and put on a Joni Mitchel album, which Jimmi and I had fallen asleep to one evening. George had developed quite a passion for Joni, and it only took one play of *Both Sides Now* before he was in tears. I then played all the sad songs I knew on my sax and the Clubbing Lunatics soon joined George blubbing on the settee. It wasn't long before the Witch had had enough with all the weeping and wailing and decided to change the music and the mood. Joni was out and Gerry Rafferty was in. George drew out some large spotted handkerchiefs from his pockets and everyone blew their noses, the Lunatics with loud trumpeting noises. Soon we were all singing along with Gerry, "Don't you worry, don't you whine 'cause if you get wrong you'll get it right next time." I took a deep breathe, maybe if there was a next time I would get it right.

...

I continued to try and find someone to play with, who would be fun and happy to practice with me, Jimmi didn't like practising, while Mad Mary was too busy, and I'm not sure that two saxes playing together was ideal. I decided to ask Faantastic Bob, who was always incredibly enthusiastic about everything. I'd been reminded of him when I bumped into his wife, Bev, at the local supermarket, a key place for social interaction and weird happenings in my life. Right by the shelves of baked beans Bev had forgiven me for some crime I'd committed a couple of years previously, although I was still none the wiser about what my misdemeanour had been. I had been trying to find some chilli beans when she had appeared dragging some huge bottles of drinking water around the end of the aisle where I had been looking. She gave me a big smile and we shared a hug and I'd taken it as a sign I was welcome to go around their house and play music. Misunderstandings happen and I was just glad the unpleasantness was over, whatever had caused it.

Bob had moved since I'd last visited him and downsized, much to his disgust. He still had his music room and regaled me with the latest misadventures of the Muddy River Boys, who had now reformed, and been round to his house for a practice and some bickering. After Bob finished his story he then played a delightful new tune he'd made up on his banjo, before picking up his bass. I knew it was going to be hard for Bob to play along to the tunes I'd chosen, so I bought my laptop and backing tracks to help give him some guidance. I used to play with him and Jay quite a lot, but without Jay to hold us together we rapidly disintegrated. After two hours of trying, and probably playing the worse version of *Aint no Sunshine* ever in history, I realised that playing Jazz with Bob was not working, for me or him.

We finished off with a few tunes on guitar and violin. It was the first time I'd played violin for weeks and trying to play something over my shoulder, rather than straight in front of me, felt totally unnatural. Eventually I coaxed some accompaniment to Bob's guitar out of it, but I was shocked how after playing the violin for five years it felt like all that experience had vanished and I was left with something I just imagined. Musically it had not been a great evening, the search for someone to play sax with would have to continue and I wondered whether I could still play the violin.

I dropped by to see Jay, only taking my violin, to see if it was still the unfamiliar object I had last played at Bobs. With Jay it all seemed to work fine and the old tunes were comforting and pleasing. "Think a bit of a break has done your playing good," he said sounding surprised. It might have been that or maybe it was just nice to feel relaxed and play with someone that enjoyed the tunes as much as I did.

Jay was now in his new home, renting a small cottage not far from Dolwen which seemed ideal for him. Outside was bright, with fields leading up to the rugged Welsh hills on the horizon, inside the cottage was warm, so warm in fact the windows had to open all the time, a favourable contrast to the large cold austerity of the house at Dolwen. He also had a new vehicle, the "Stealth" car, as he called it. It was a sort of suburban 'run around' and was so incongruous with the image of Jay I was used to, it made me laugh when I first saw him in it. Some things hadn't changed, though, and piles of boxes occupied every space as I came through the door. I wondered how after being there for some weeks he could not feel the urge to unpack them, or least stack them so he could use the lounge, but things like that never seemed to bother him.

They did bother me and before I left I couldn't resist helping him unpack some stuff and make some space, just for old time sake. We knew each other so well and shared some of the old jokes as we sorted through the boxes. Finally I left, wondering when I'd see him again. In a couple of weeks he would be leaving for America to pursue a new dream, and love, someone he'd never met. I hoped he would find what he was looking for and he would hold on to his new found happiness and peace of mind.

Harmony in my own life remained elusive, even an innocent trip to the cinema proved hazardous. I had gone to see a film about Martin Luther King's civil rights march from Selma to Montgomery. The cinema was quite empty but I spotted a couple of ladies I knew from the village and as I went to over to say 'Hello' I asked if they minded if I sat with them, which they said was fine. I soon began to regret my decision as I felt very strongly that the lady I was sitting by didn't want me be next to her, but it felt too awkward to move away. I had to endure the movie feeling rather disconcerted and as the final credits rolled I leapt up with relief, I was twenty minutes late picking my son up and wanted to leave quickly. I picked up my bag, and said "Goodbye", and as I started to leave she leant across.

"Jess I just have to say I finally finished your book and I am very uncomfortable with it. You should have been much more careful disguising the other characters; you can't just use people like that." She looked really pained and I was taken aback. She'd had the book since the previous summer and had reported enthusiastically back on Part 1 suggesting I try to get it more widely published. I guess she found the more personal nature of Part 2 disturbing and knew some of the characters I had mentioned. It all seemed a long time ago and I barely thought about it anymore, I was already well into my present book.

"I'm really sorry you feel like that. I'm happy to talk about it but I can't now I have to pick by son up." I left feeling shocked that that I had upset her.

I got home and called Crazy who was also puzzled, "The book is essentially about you and you are the most inoffensive person. I don't know why she would feel like that. Don't worry about it, get some sleep." I couldn't sleep and did worry about it. I spoke to some other friends; Jonah was level headed about it, said he loved my book, but could see that living in a small village some people might be upset by it, Katie looked askance "It's just a book about your journey of discovery, you just told it as it was."

I read my reviews on Amazon and tried to feel reassured that my book had been read in the spirit I had envisioned when I wrote it. I had felt concerned writing about some of the events, and had tried to edit the most potentially offending bits without completely losing all substance. As I had originally hoped to get it accepted by a professional publisher I didn't think it would be read by people who would know the characters anyway. I sat down and composed a letter to the troubled lady.

Dear Delyth,

Thank you for your honesty about your feelings about my book when I met you at the cinema on Tuesday night. I sensed your discomfort when I sat next to you and was unclear as to why that was. I am happy to meet and discuss this any time but I thought I would write first as this is usually a better way for me to collect my thoughts.

When I wrote my book it was certainly not intended to cause offence or upset anybody. As a biography it is mostly about me, initially about my musical journey, which was supposed to end at chapter ten, but as events unfolded at the camp, I decided to take the advice offered to me in chapter eleven and write more personally. As someone who is very shy and feels uncomfortable at most social gatherings this felt quite intimidating at first, but gradually it became an opportunity to express myself and try to make some sense of what was happening in my life. As I was writing contemporaneously I had no idea of how things would unfold and I suppose it became like keeping a diary. I attempted to represent events fairly and not be judgemental; emotional frailties, stress and misunderstandings sometimes make us act in ways that are less than heroic, myself included.

As I tried to be open and truthful about myself in my writing I made little attempt to disguise other characters, I wanted to understand people's reactions to me, not judge or condemn them. I do not gossip, or scandalise, and feel that most people are fundamentally good. I realise being objective can be difficult so I had three friends, who knew everybody else mentioned in the book, read it before publication and give me their opinions. One of these was 'Jay' who featured the most and didn't have a problem with what I wrote about him so I hoped this was an indication that I had also presented others in a fair way.

It was now 18 months since the point at which I finished it and a year since publishing, and life has moved on. As far as I am aware not many people have read it, and disappointingly those that have were more interested in me than my music, but I guess that is human nature. I'm sorry for your discomfort surrounding people that you know; unfortunately life is less than perfect. Even Martin Luther King had his weaknesses, as portrayed in last night's film. We all make mistakes and I'm really sorry if I have upset anyone.

I accept that what I wrote is from my point of view, and others may see things differently, but I have tried to be honest about how I felt and acted, and as a literary and musical expression of my feelings I am proud of my book and CD. Honest expression sometimes involves touching on things that we may find uncomfortable and I guess people will read and listen and take what they want to see and hear. My mum plays my CD all the time because she says it makes her happy and she has read my book a number of times because she says it's the first time she feels she has known anything about me. Perhaps it was naive of me to expect others to feel the same but that was my intention behind my work.

I hope this clarifies things a little, even if you don't agree with my perspective. I respect your opinion and will be more cautious with my next book in view of what you have said. Please call by any time for coffee. It would be lovely to see you, but I understand if you would rather not.

Jesse

Feeling misjudged by her comments and blue about my love life, I decided it was time to take a vacation and put some distance between myself and recent events.

Chapter 10. Vacation

Laughter is an instant vacation. (Milton Berle)

I packed up the van; there wasn't a lot of space and only room for necessities, which meant instruments and a waterproof. Outside there was a bit of commotion and I looked up a huge black carriage drew up, pulled by six white horses and driven by two coachman. They hauled on the reigns and the horses stopped, chewing on their bits and shaking their heads as they rested. The carriage door opened and George leapt out.

"Thought we'd come with you, I could do with a break myself."

"Nice coach. I see you are travelling in moderate style as usual," I said, with a sense of irony.

"Yes, it's the one I had purpose built, modelled on Napoleons own carriage, I used it to travel to Geneva when I went into exile."

"I'm not going into exile, only to Anglesey," I said, wondering if there might be some similarities. I looked inside the coach. George was a notorious over-packer, but it looked like he had excelled himself for this trip. The interior was crammed full of chests, books, clothes, pictures and furniture, as well as a dog, a peacock in a cage, and a monkey on leash. The peacock was mewing, the monkey chattering and the dog growling. On a table a full tea service was laid out and a servant was pouring tea into the bone china cups, ignoring the commotion. A rather pale looking young man sat wide eyed in the corner, transfixed by the peacock. George extended his hand towards him.

"My personal physician, Dr John Polidori, Pollydolly." Pollydolly smiled at me weakly before his eyes were drawn back to the mewing peacock.

"Also my valet, Fletcher," George introduced the tall austere servant. "Will you be taking tea with us Jesse?"

"No thanks, I need to get going, safe journey and good luck," I said, extending my wishes more to Pollydolly than George, the physician already looked close to a nervous breakdown. Shaking my head I went back to the van. Eleanor was sat in the front wearing a yellow sou'wester and the Lunatics were in the back with matching sou'westers and their clubs. The weather had been shocking and everyone was prepared for the worse. I started up the engine and headed north, speculating when George would catch us up.

I was soon in the heart of Snowdonia and had an urged to do some mountaineering. I stopped at a farm at the bottom of Tryfan; it was probably twenty five years since I last climbed it, but I recognised its' bristly back, arched like a dinosaur above Llyn Ogwen. As the sun went down the weather looked set fair for the following day, the moon rose and the black spines lay in wait.

The morning dawned with perfect blues skies and the arrival of George. I stepped out of the van to find his carriage with the horses all lathered up and the coachmen doing their best to calm them down. "Terrible journey," remarked one, "broke a wheel and axel." I knocked on the carriage door and Fletcher invited me inside, the atmosphere was rather fetid, a mixture of peacock, monkey and dog. Bits of fur and feathers were scattered around. It looked like the animals had been fighting. George was tending Pollydolly, who was laid across one of the seats covered in a tartan blanket, while George dabbed his head with a cloth. He looked up as I entered, "Touch of the vapours I think," he said frowning, "he took a turn for the worse after the axel broke. Do you think I should apply some of these?" he asked, shaking a jar of rather repulsive looking leeches at me.

"Probably not," I said "but maybe you should let the animals out, it's a bit crowded in here." The peacock mewed loudly in agreement; it was desperate to find a mate before it lost all its feathers to the dog.

"Nonsense," said George "animals are excellent company don't you think Pollydolly?" Pollydolly groaned and seemed to be having a relapse.

"Maybe I should try the leeches," said George frowning, "a few leeches never hurt anybody."

"Actually George I think it was a bit of over enthusiastic bleeding by the quacks that finally killed you down in Greece. Blood is a precious commodity, why not just open some windows and let some good Welsh air in?" I suggested, feeling a little sorry for Pollydolly who was at the mercy of Georges not very accomplished nursing skills.

"Very well," said George flinging open some windows, "I think we should go for a walk and leave Pollydolly to rest."

"Good idea." I agreed, and we set off, over a style and up a ridge towards the Glyders. It was a brilliant morning, the light had an intense, piercing Alpine quality about it, and as I got higher there was even the odd patch of snow in sheltered pockets. By nine o'clock I was climbing in shirt sleeves and George praised the magnificent day with his wonderful poetry as we strode along.

My joy was in the Wilderness; to breathe
The difficult air of the iced mountain's top
Where the birds dare not build, nor insect wing
Flit o'er the herbless granite; or to plunge
Into the torrent, and to roll along
On the swift whirl of the new breaking wave
Of river-stream, or ocean, in their flow.
In these my early strength exalted

Now in my fifties, I was hardly in my early strength, but my joy was still in the wilderness and I related to George's romantic view of the sublime. I felt truly blessed that I had good health to enjoy it, and legs that carried me where ever I wanted to go. The Lunatics had now joined us, still proudly wearing their sou'westers, and occasionally disappearing in the peat bog that surrounded us, only their yellow headwear staying above water. There was a buzzing noise overhead and Eleanor flew by in a micro light. It was the closest she would go to riding a broomstick. As I picked out a route through the rocks and tussocks I was filled with happiness and in less than two hours we reached the top of Glyder Fach. Until then we had met no one, but ahead was an imposing man, wearing thick red cape and a crown, sitting astride a white charger.

"What the devil?" spluttered George.

"King Arthur," I said without hesitation. "I'm afraid you're on the wrong mountain," I said to him, "you're supposed to be over there on Tryfan," and pointed behind me. I knew this after a late visit to the toilet, the previous evening. As I had ventured from the van I had noticed a porta cabin, much closer than going up to the farm house for ablutions, and thought it must contain a toilet. Sure enough I opened the door and an automatic light came on to reveal one. I was just about to step into it when a voice behind me said, "Are you looking for the camp toilets?" I jumped around in surprise to see an officious looking woman standing there wearing fluorescent jacket. We both stared at the toilet in front of us and I wondered whether she was being obtuse. "Yes," I said and took a step towards it. "You can't use that one she said slightly threateningly, it's for the film crew. Clearly she was mad, who would lurk around at eleven o'clock at night guarding a toilet for a film crew.

She could see I didn't believe her, "They haven't turned up yet," she said trying to offer an explanation.

"What are you filming," I asked suspiciously.

"A film about King Arthur."

"Is all that matting to do with you?" I asked, having been wondering why there was an area of bog, about the size of half a football pitch, covered in plastic matting.

"Yes it's so the heavy vehicles don't sink," she explained.

Well at least that made sense, "So are you filming at the farm?"

"No, on Tryfan."

Now I knew that Arthur got around a bit, but had not appreciated Tryfan was one of his haunts. I wasn't going to wrestle the lady to use the toilet; she was much bigger than me, so I stumbled on up to the farm to use their small dark offering. Anyway, that's how I knew it was Arthur on the horse before us, and that he was on the wrong mountain.

"Hell's teeth!" cursed Arthur, "have you any idea how busy it is being a legend?"

"No," I said.

"I have to be down in Cornwall this evening," he said rather huffily.

"No problem," I shrugged, "judging by all the hoof imprints you've left around the country it should be a doddle.

"Ummp," he threw his cape dramatically over one shoulder, his horse tossed his mane and they flounced off in the direction of Tryfan.

We in turn scrambled over the jumble of boulders at the top of Glyder Fach, and then down the north side onto Blwch Tryfan. My eye problems made negotiating the rocks and steep path problematic, but the ascent up the southern flank of Tryfan was easier, and it wasn't long before I was on the summit, marked by the huge stone monoliths known as Adam and Eve. It is a tradition to climb up and jump from one to another. I'd done it many years ago and found it rather scary, and that was when I could still judge distances accurately. It's one of those things that looks even worse, once you're standing on the top, and realise that if you misjudge it you risk either falling off the near side and smashing your head open on the surrounding boulders, or alternatively, tumbling hundreds of feet down the shear drop on the far side.

When we arrived there was a group of walkers trying to psyche each other up to making the jump, so far no one had got further than standing on one block, giving a whimper, and climbing back down again. Ugg, Nugg, Fump, and Wump, were not so intimidated and after a series of synchronised leaps, where they wacked clubs as they flew by in mid-air, they then successfully executed cartwheels and summersaults. I left them to it, I wasn't feeling that brave, and decided it was time to leave the summit crowds and climb back down to the valley floor.

I had a vague memory that the best descent route was to drop down onto a path that traversed the side of the mountain, called Heather Terrace. I couldn't remember how to find it but assumed it would be easy enough. I went along the ridge a bit further before seeing a gulley that looked an easy way down. Unfortunately it was one of those gulley's that sucked you in before you realised you'd rather not be there. It became steeper and more exposed and I found myself gulping down great lumps of fear in my throat. I knew it was a bad place to be as there were people coming up from below using helmets and ropes. By then I was fully committed to the route and started doing those climbing moves which betray the panic within, thumping hand holds and kicking at footholds, in case they deceived me and I fell to an unpleasant death below.

It was with a huge sigh of relief I finally arrived on something which resembled Heather Terrace and scrambled along it rounding a corner to meet a cheery faced gentleman.

"Ah you look like you know what you're doing," he said brightly.

"Not really," I said grimly, "you should have seen where I've just come from."

"Err do you know the way down?" he said looking a bit disappointed, "it's just my wife's a bit sacred and is reluctant to go any further," he pointed to an ashen faced woman clinging onto a rock.

"Well I haven't been up here for a long time but it looks like it leads on down there," I said pointing to some worn rocks, "I'll take a look." Cautiously I went to the end of the slope and peered down, I could see people coming up from below. "Yes this is the right way," I shouted back, relieved as much for myself as the worried gentleman who'd led his wife astray. The rest of the descent was less dramatic, although rather long and tiring, George joined Eleanor in the micro light and took the easy option down, while the Lunatics bounced and rolled their way to the bottom, with sickening thuds and groans. I wished I could join them, but their bones were much thicker and stronger than mine and I would have been in pieces.

When I finally arrived back at camp George was having tea, sitting outside his carriage sunning himself with Pollydolly, who had perked up a little and was eating Welsh cakes. I needed a shower, there were salt crystals all over my face. I went up the farm to take one and it was only after I took all my clothes off I realised I needed a token, but couldn't find the farmer to obtain one. I wrapped myself in a towel and went back to the van, ate a stack of food, before going back up to the farm to try again, without success. Disgruntled I decided to head on up to Anglesey that night and find a campsite where I could get a shower. I packed up, waved to George, and set off.

It was a beautiful evening, but by the time I got to Bethesda a thick sea mist was rolling in and the sun had disappeared. I put my headlights on and drove on into the gloom until suddenly the huge concrete arches of the Menai suspension bridge appeared, indicating I was crossing onto Anglesey, or Ynys Mon, to give its Welsh name. The gapping chasm of the bridge swallowed me up and when I emerged on the other side the easiest thing seemed to keep following the A5 to Holyhead and try to find the small coastal resort, Trearddur, which was close by. Janey, my work colleague, had told me this was nice to visit, but when I finally arrived it looked like everywhere else on Anglesey, featureless and grey. There appeared to be no coastline and since most of the houses were white, there were few identifiable outlines of anything. The only thing that indicated life was the constant beat of a fog horn.

Eventually I found a caravan site, rather soulless, but at least it had a shower. Gratefully I paid, parked and entered the shower block. Due to my haphazard meanderings around Anglesey it had now been over two hours since I'd left the farm and I was looking forward to getting clean. I stripped off and got out my toilet bag only find that I'd left my soap and shampoo back in the toilet block at the farm. It was just one of those evenings. I wrapped a towel around me, got out the shower, went over to the sinks, filled my hand with soap from a dispenser and dashed back into the shower, it would have to do.

I got back to the van feeling cleaner, although not completely satisfied by my experience. By midnight George had arrived and parked his coach next to my van. He had made good progress, but was not happy.

"This infernal fog, damn weather reminds me of that summer of 1816 in Geneva," he remarked grimly.

Due to a volcanic eruption it had certainly not been a pleasant summer that year when George had arrived at the Villa Diodati, following his hurried departure from the shores of England into exile. Behind him was the scandal of separation from his wife after only a year, rumours of cruelty, incest, and homosexuality, and with the latter being a capital offence, there wasn't a lot of incentive for him to return. Unfortunately scandal is often difficult to escape, especially in George's case, and in Geneva he found Claire Clairmont awaiting him, pregnant with his child. Somehow during the turbulence of his separation and exodus, George had fitted in a short dalliance with the lady, and the consequences were evident to see.

More up lifting than this indiscretion, was the appearance of Percy Shelly, and Claire Clairmont's step sister, Mary Goodwin, soon to be Mary Shelley. The four of them spent the inclement summer at George's villa, passing the time telling ghost stories. Mary Shelley's would eventually be published as *Frankenstein*, while Pollydolly later used George's fragment story as inspiration for writing *The Vampyre*, forerunner of the romantic vampire genre.

"Let's tell ghost stories," said George excitedly, obviously remembering that happy time and cheering up at the thought of relieving the experience.

"I don't think we can top your previous efforts," I said, as Frankenstein's monster and a vampire peeped through the carriage window, "but I would like to know why Mary Shelley's sub-title for *Frankenstein* was *The Modern Prometheus*."

"Ah, yes, most people have forgotten that with the passage of time and those ridiculous films. You see Prometheus was a Titan, charged by Zeus to create mankind, which he did, sculpting them from clay and water and giving them knowledge. Against the will of Zeus he gave them the gift of fire, stealing it from Mount Olympus. For this Zeus sentenced him to eternal punishment, fixing him to a rock at Caucasus, where each day an eagle pecked out his liver. Unfortunately because he was immortal he suffered the same fate every day."

"Harsh," I said, feeling sorry for Prometheus.

"Well, the God of Thunder is not known for his measured temperament," George reasoned, "but don't worry he was eventually rescued by Hercules. Anyway, Prometheus represents the risk of unintended consequences which may happen when we're being creative, with Victor Frankenstein's monster being a 'modern' representation of that principle. It can apply to any form of creative ideas, even writing. Sometimes when you're totally focused on what you're doing its easy to lose sight of the effects your work may have in the future.

"Yes, that's true, you never know how people will react to your ideas," I agreed.

In the background I could hear screams from the toilet block, footsteps, and people running. I wondered what Frankenstein's monster and the vampire were up to. Dark shadows passed by the window, along with snatches of frantic whispers and scared laughter. It was definitely time for bed.

In the morning I could still hear the fog horn blaring, however the gloom was definitely lifting and by the time I'd had breakfast and gone for a walk, the coastline had appeared. It was pretty, but failed to capture my imagination, I had no desire to stay and wanted to leave the sanitised conditions of the caravan park as soon as possible. As soon as I got back I packed up and left. It was Bank Holiday Monday and all roads seemed to lead to the retail parks that surrounded Holyhead. I visited the same one several times before I finally escaped and then sat in a carpark overlooking the sea, unclear where to go.

"I think you should go down to Ynys Llanddwyn, and visit Dwynwen, it's nice and peaceful down there," Eleanor advised sitting in the passenger seat, gazing out to sea with me.

"Dwynwen?"

"Saint Dwynwen, lovely girl, knows all about affairs of the heart."

I shrugged, "If you say so, it's has to be better than sitting in this carpark."

I headed back down South to the village of Newborough and found a small field on the outskirts to camp in. I took out my fiddle and played for a while but didn't think it was fair to play my sax there and disturb the other campers, so I drove down to the peninsula hoping to find an isolated spot. It was late afternoon, and the peaceful pine forest I passed through boded well, however when I arrived at the carpark it contained at least a thousand people and a burger van. My sax would have to wait, the easiest way to escape a tourist hotspot like this was to walk, the usual rule of thumb being at least ninety percent of people never venture further than five hundred meters from their car. Sure enough ten minutes later I was by myself, walking through the long cool shadows of the pines, treading on the soft needles that had dropped onto the path from the branches above.

Threads of vapour threaded through the forest, from the encroaching sea mist, giving it a mysterious feel. Eleanor, Ugg, Nugg, Wump and Fump had now joined me, the Lunatics seemed edgy, swinging their clubs around anxiously and muttering between themselves. Suddenly two ancient Druids popped out from behind the trees, startling all of us. They had long cloaks, wild hair and beards, and waved their arms to the heavens shouting dreadful imprecations. According to the Roman historian, Tacitus, this chilling Druid practice momentarily paralysed the Roman armies of Paulinus when they invaded the Druid stronghold of Mona (Ynys Mon) in AD 60. Urged on by their commanders the soldiers quickly recovered their wits and massacred the opposition. The Druids had a terrifying reputation for ritual human sacrifice and nobody wanted to be their next victim.

The Lunatics also decided that the Druids weren't as scary as they looked and charged towards them. The Druids took one look at the four men thick clubs and wisely took flight, disappearing into the dark interior of the woods. As their shouts became faint I left the path to walk on the beach, unable to see much except my feet, until suddenly the mist cleared and Llanddwyn peninsula loomed ahead. Although occasionally an island on high tides it was now dry and I walked out past the pillow lavas, formed by primordial volcanic eruptions under the cold water, and then carried on along the narrow strip of land, out towards the sea. I turned to Eleanor who was walking beside me.

"So, tell me about Saint Dwynwen."

"Well," she said, "of course there are a number of versions of her tale, but here's mine, a typical mix of romance and tragedy. Dwynwen was a princess, who lived a long time ago in the medieval kingdom of Brecon, and was the fairest of all the daughters of King Brychan Brycheiniog. She fell in love with a local man, Maelon. Unfortunately, for the sake of a political alliance her father had already betrothed her to another. When Maelon found out he raped Dwynwen, brutally ending their innocent love. Distraught Dwynwen prayed to God that she would forget her feelings for Maelon and her wish was granted. An angel appeared in the night giving her a potion for forgetfulness, and also turned Maelon into a block of ice."

"Result!"

"Quite," said the Witch, sharply, "don't interrupt. The compassionate Dwynwen then asked to be granted a further three wishes; that Maelon be thawed, that she remain celibate for the rest of her life and that she be allowed to safeguard the fate of true lovers throughout time. Her wishes were granted and in return she dedicated the rest of her life to God. She became a nun, set up a convent on Llanddwyn Island and became the patron saint of lovers. Saint Dwynwens Day, the Welsh equivalent of Saint Valentine's day, is celebrated on January the twenty fifth and pilgrimages are made to the holy well of Dwynwen, where sacred fish are said to predict whether love will succeed."

"Well I guess becoming a nun, and achieving sainthood, is one way to deal with your love life when it all goes pear shaped," I said flippantly, "gets rid of all the heart ache and avoids difficult decision making." I looked at her suspiciously, "You're not suggesting I become a nun are you?"

"Well, I think sainthood is beyond you," she said archly, "but I guess we can forget the nun thing too."

I pulled a face at her, by now we were approaching the ruins of the ancient church which had been supposedly built on the site of Dwynwens monastery. All that remained was a huge arched window in which George was seated chatting to an ethereal looking lady next to him. Eleanor waved at them.

"You hoo, Dwynwen, George," she called.

They waved back. I could now see that George was wearing his Albanian national costume, which he had procured during his first tour of Europe, and was looking very suave. I could also see from his body language and hear by the tone of his voice he was flirting with Dwynwen. George was flirting with a saint and a former nun at that! We reached them and George gave me a wink, "Every woman is a mystery to be solved," he said with a dazzling smile, before having the decency to look a little abashed and assume a look of deference more appropriate to the occasion. Dwynwen was looking a little pink and flustered, and it was apparent that no one was safe from George's charm.

"As I was saying, Dwynwen," he continued with the conversation he'd just broken off from, there are only four questions of value in life; What is sacred? Of what is the spirit made? What is worth living for, and what is worth dying for?" He paused slightly for effect, before answering his own question, "The answer to each is the same: only love."

Dwynwen went all shimmery and I tried to avoid snorting at George's blatant plagiarism of Johnny Depp's lines from the film Don Juan DeMarco.

"All you need is love?" I said raising an eyebrow.

"All you need is love," George answered dreamily.

At this point the two Druids, I had seen earlier in the woods, reappeared with some more Druid friends, and spontaneously started singing the Beatles classic hit. "Love, love, love," they all sang, swaying together in unison while waving sprigs of mistletoe above their heads. They had obviously made up with the Lunatics who were the band members for the group, Nugg was on drums, while the others had guitars and each wore a mop top wig. They were doing quite a good impersonation of The Fab Four, Ugg even had the John Lennon glasses. From their position in the arch window, Eleanor, Dwynwen and George sang along with the Druid choir, providing the harmonies, and soon it felt like the whole area had turned into one huge love in.

"All you need is love?" I repeated to myself, if only life were that simple. I wasn't sure which I related to most, George's rather naive views on love in his present reincarnation as a hippy, or his more scathing take on the condition, in his poem Don Juan;

And that's enough, for love is vanity,
  Selfish in its beginning and end,
Except where't is a mere insanity,
  A maddening spirit which would strive to blend
Itself with beauty's frail inanity,
  On which the passion's self seems to depend:
And hence some heathenish philosophers
  Make love the main spring of the universe.

Upon reflection I seem to be suffering from the insanity version and wished its 'maddening spirit' would leave me. The best I could achieve at the moment was walk away from the Welsh version of Woodstock and returned to the carpark. When I got back it was nearly deserted and I picked up my sax, practised some scales and then some tunes, wishing I had someone to play with. I stood with my back against a tree trunk and Bird appeared with his band. He was playing *Lover Man (Oh where can you be)* in that soulful way he had. I found it the most poignant of songs and I sang along with the tune in my head.

I don't know why but I'm feeling so sad,
I long to try something I've never had
Never had no kissing
Oh, what I've been missing
Lover man, oh, where can you be

The night is cold and I'm so all alone
I'd give my soul just to call you my own
Got a moon above me
But no one to love me
Lover man, oh, where can you be

I've heard it said
That the thrill of romance
Can be like a heavenly dream
I'd go to bed with a prayer
That you make love to me
Strange as it seems

Someday we'll meet
And you'll dry all my tears
Then whisper sweet
Little things in my ear
Hugging and a-kissing
Oh, what I've been missing
Lover man, oh, where can you be

The last note of Birds sax died away, the vibrato filled with longing for the lover man, and I wondered how he played the sax so expressively. He read my thoughts and spoke, *"You've got to learn your instrument. Then, you practice, practice, practice. And then, when you finally get up on the bandstand, forget all that and just wail."* I thought it would not only take a lot of practice, but also a lot of pain to make a sax wail like that. The light faded and I drove back to the campsite in silence.

The next day dawned brightly and I went back to the carpark. There were much fewer visitors around and I played my sax, undisturbed, in a deserted corner under the whispering pines. In the afternoon I walked back out to the end of the peninsula to look at the relics and views in peace, and gaze across the sea to Bardsey Island, before wandering back. George had parked his enormous carriage next my van and I could hear him shouting and the dog barking. The reason for the uproar soon became apparent, the peacock had escaped, aided and abetted by Pollydolly.

"I merely thought it would like to stretch its legs," said Pollydolly contritely.

"Yes, but not at break neck speed being chased by a dog." said George, sounding cross.

The dog sat guiltily in the shade with a feather hanging out its mouth, whilst further evidence of his crime littered the ground about. I began to pick the feathers up.

"Any idea where it went?" I asked.

"Last seen heading that way," George pointed deeper into the woods.

"Oh dear," I said but secretly thinking the peacock was better off, "do you mind if I keep these?" I asked waving the tail feathers at him.

"No," said George looking distracted.

"I'm heading back to the mountains now, maybe see you down there?"

"Maybe," said George. "Come on Pollydolly, its time to form a search party."

Pollydolly got up, not very enthusiastically, and trailed after George into the woods. I got into my van, carefully putting the feathers on the back seat thinking they would look good in a vase in the bathroom, before starting up the engine and heading back to the mainland.

As it was evening I thought it would probably be easiest to stay at the same farm I had a few nights before, but when I drew up at the entrance there was an official standing at it, and in the background a bustle of frenzied activity focused around putting up a huge marquee. It appeared the film crew had finally arrived.

"I'm sorry the farm is closed to campers," the official smiled pleasantly, but firmly. Disappointed I carried on down the road to Capel Curig, passing Arthur on his white charger, still looking for the film crew. I waved and Arthur responded by making the horse theatrically rear up while he pointed his sword toward the setting sun, he was such a drama King. A little further on I spotted another farm without a film crew occupying it and pulled in. On the opposite side of the road the distinctive outline of Moel Siabod loomed above me, beckoning, it seemed like a good walk for the following day.

After a good night's sleep I started early, meeting the farmer as I walked out. He looked like he'd been hewn from the rocks of Moel Siabod itself and imparted to me his local wisdom on the mountain. "The mountain with the largest base in Europe," he said authoritatively, which was new information to me. By the time I'd reached the summit, via a rather deviant route on the south side, I didn't doubt him. I felt like I'd walked a substantial part of its circumference, whilst falling into a lot of it's bogs.

There was no one else about and I took a picture of my feet, standing on top of the trig point, before making my way back down. The descent was quick, it was only early afternoon by the time I reached the van, and feeling tired I decided to head for home. I arrived back, unpacked, put the peacock feathers in the vase in the bathroom and took a long hot shower. It had been a short break, but I felt fulfilled by all the things I'd done and seen, and the new people I'd met. George and the others arrived back the following day, having never found the peacock, and as far as know it's still living free in the pine forest of Newborough, minus a few tail feathers.

Chapter 11. The Curse of the Tiger Cat

Life is a tragedy when seen in close-up, but a comedy in long shot. (Charlie Chaplin)

When I got back from Anglesey I went round to see Jimmi to talk about the saxophone CD I wanted to make. I was impressed how good the recordings were that he had made with me a couple of months previously, and felt that having had more practise time on the horn, we could achieve something even better. It wouldn't be like the last CD I had, to go with a book with links and everything, it would just be "art for art sake".

Jimmi said he needed a laptop to do it and saw one on EBay that would do the job. I bought it for him to set up as part of the recording deal we made, as I tried to keep contact with him on a business level and maintain my distance. He said he couldn't be the hundred percent kinda guy I wanted and despite staying away from him for the last few weeks I realised that I still had to guard my feelings carefully, so that I felt less off balance by his unexplained absences and concerns about his health. His breathing was now so bad he could barely move around, and even he felt he should try and give up smoking.

Strangely Jimmi seemed to be able to go from needing constant rest, to being able to play at a music night or disappearing to see friends at the drop of a hat, which was what, happened a few days after I returned from Anglesey. He went to Liverpool and then down to London, to record with Daz, and then went up north to recover, sending me the occasional health update, with recovery one day followed by sudden relapses. You never knew when Jimmi might return, but suddenly he did, nearly on his knees from problems with his heart. I went straight round to his flat, with a meal I'd cooked, and carried all his bags and guitars up for him. Jimmi was grateful and when I got back from work the following day, he messaged me, inviting me over for tea.

I went around to his flat and found his friend Roz visiting on her way back from her travels in her van. Jimmi was complaining about chest pain, and I'd said I'd cook, but he insisted on doing it, even though he had sit down. Once he had finished the stack of pancakes I took them through to share with Roz. She seemed like a fun lady but I didn't stay long as Jimmi was groaning about how tired he was and that he needed to rest.

When I got up the following morning and saw he hadn't replied to text I sent him the previous evening, I was puzzled, when I looked on Facebook and saw he hadn't been active for twelve hours I was alarmed. For Jimmi to be at home and not on Facebook, however bad he was feeling, was unheard of. I phoned, texted, and messaged him, but there was no reply.

I was going for a run and I decided the easiest thing was to call by and check he was okay. I raced up the back steps and hammered on the door. There was no answer and unusually it was locked. I banged louder and debated about calling an ambulance before running round and trying the front door buzzer... nothing... I kept pressing while contemplating what I should do. Suddenly the income was picked up and Jimmi spoke.

"Hello?"

"It's Jesse, are you all right? You haven't answered my messages, or been on Facebook since yesterday when I left, and you seemed so ill I was wondering whether I should call ambulance."

"No I just needed to rest," he replied in a feeble voice.

"Can you let me in?"

"I'm alright."

I insisted, I wanted to see him for my own eyes having becoming increasingly worried over the previous two hours. He let me in and stood there looking angry in his dressing gown, "I thought the bailiffs were at the door."

"Look I'm really sorry but you've been so ill recently I thought you'd had a heart attack."

"Well I haven't and I've just gone from deep rest to wide awake, which is not what I needed."

He went through to the kitchen and started to fill the kettle up. I felt guilty that I had disturbed him and started to apologise again, upset that I done the wrong thing despite the best of intensions.

"Why don't you let me make you a cup of tea while you go and lie down and I'll bring it to you?" I reached for the kettle.

"Look, I'm alright," Jimmi started to raise his voice, "you're just making things worse, look how my hand is shaking."

He started dramatically shaking his hand that he was holding the kettle with. It was obviously put on, but he was certainly getting himself into a state and wanted me to leave. I left ran back home feeling distressed by his aggressive reaction towards my concerns for him. I wondered why he had acted in such a way. Jimmi sent me a text reassuring me that he just was feeling drained and needed to rest and I tried to believe him.

Two days later there was a Spanish fiesta at Shady Grove and I was still feeling wounded by Jimmi's angry scene, and not really keen to go. Ally called me and persuaded me, saying it would do me good to have a drink. Perhaps it would and I arrived mid-afternoon and had soon imbibed quite a few drinks, as had Ally. A full on girly confessional followed. In vino veritas, indeed.

My mood was slightly better after my disclosure and we went back to join the party. By now Roz and Jimmi's mate, Dave, had arrived, but Jimmi was feeling too ill to come. I was talking to Dave, who I had met previously, while Ally chatted to Roz. She soon found out that Roz had been staying at Jimmi's flat and had been the reason that Jimmi was so anxious for me to leave the morning I had called around. Ally also knew that Jimmi had been juggling seeing his two old girlfriends, Jane and Tess, again. Burdened down by all the confessions she been hearing, Ally decided the situation was past saying a few Hail Mary's and that honesty was the best policy for those involved.

The party continued while I gradually absorbed the leakage of information, considering it in the light of recent events and whether I could trust anything Jimmi said. It was not surprising how fragile his health had been over the last few months, the stress of it all on his heart must have been enormous.

I felt hurt by his subterfuge and I realised my feelings about him made me vulnerable to being used. Considering everything I decided it was best if I didn't see him anymore. To reduce the possibility of this happening I needed to burn all bridges and chop up all rowing boats that were lying around. This meant retrieving the lap top and amp batteries he had of mine in case I was tempted to do any music with him.

I was concerned about what Jimmi's reaction might be. Ally said she get them for me, which didn't seem fair, and in the end we agreed to go together, hoping that with Roz and Dave would be there and diffuse the situation. I picked up Ally, who still had a banging headache from the previous night and was drinking hair of the dog. We were both nervous; I couldn't bear confrontations of any kind, and was grateful when we arrived at Jimmi's flat to be let in by Roz. We went through into the sitting room where Dave was sitting awkwardly; he was one of Jimmi's oldest friends and looked like he wished he was somewhere else. Jimmi was standing looking angry. Fortunately Ally was right behind me and I couldn't run out of the room. I could hear her muttering a reassuring mantra of "It's not your fault", and I plucked up courage and spoke to him.

"I can't see you anymore and I want my laptop and batteries back, I don't want to do any music with you either."

"You must hate me," said Jimmi said harshly.

"No," I said puzzled, "I..." but before I could say any more Jimmi launched into a verbal attack, stabbing his finger at me, saying how it was all my fault, even managing to drag Jay into his rant. I stared at him and said nothing, there was no point in adding fuel to his fire and it was futile trying to answer his accusations, he wasn't going to listen. Eventually he dried up and there was a pause.

"Take your stuff then," he concluded, passing the lap top to me.

"Thank you," I said quietly. I turned and walked out, it was over. Outside Ally was elated by the relief that we'd completed our mission, while I felt numb, replaying the whole scene over and over again in my mind. I couldn't understand why Jimmi was so angry with me when I'd only ever tried to help him.

We got back to Shady Grove for a restorative cup of tea and both unfriended Jimmi from our Face Book accounts. A message flashed up from Face Book saying, "We're sorry you've had this experience", I laughed ironically, they didn't know the half of it, and it turned out that neither did I.

That evening, as I sat at home, mulling things over, a group message came up from Jane, to me, Tess and Roz, on FaceBook. It was a brave communication suggesting that we all made it clear to Jimmi that his recent behaviour had been unacceptable. The exchanges between us also gave a more detailed account of how events had unfolded over the past few months. When it had all been pieced together, it made me feel like I'd been involved in some black comedy. It didn't seem very funny at that point and as the revelations mounted I dragged myself through following week, barely able to sleep or eat. What I needed was to play some soothing music into my soul and that was proving to be a problem.

My sax was sick and had been for some-time, getting steadily worse until I could hardly bear to pick it up. Finally I took it back to the shop for investigations, where it turned out I'd bent the octave mechanism and needed a new part. It was such a relief to know it was the sax and not me. While it was sent away to get fixed they were able to lend me a student sax and I couldn't wait to get it home and play it. Using the mouth piece of my Selmer it sounded pretty good, and best of all I could hit every note without something strange happening.

At last I could relax and I played the Blues for hours. The sea serpents of Laocoon, wrapped around my guts, began to loosen their grip slightly. My ability to express the Blues on sax was definitely improving, probably because, as Jimmi would say, "You have to walk the Blues to play it". I wasn't sure why I felt so upset, but the whole episode seemed to have stirred up all sorts of emotions from the past and I felt as if something more profound had taken place.

There was no sign of the Witch; perhaps she had given up on me, having warned me not to make the same mistakes with Jimmi as I had with Jay. I'd played music with both of them, tried to be a good friend, and helped each of them build a home, but at some point I had crossed the friendship line. The consequences of this had been the same; neither were the close family I had once felt them to be. Jay was now more like some distant cousin, presently living in America, while it seemed like I might never speak to Jimmi again.

I didn't know how to begin explaining recent events to anybody. It was easy to pass judgement on happenings that were far more complicated than they might initially appear, however I began to chat to Roz on Facebook, and sometimes phoned her. As she had been there I didn't have to explain the background to the situation. Also the fact that I barely knew her, together with the anonymity of the phone line, made it easy to talk. Her pragmatism and humour helped and she suggested I should get out more, so when a patient excitedly told me about a new singing group in the village I decided to give it a go. Afterall singing can be a great release for emotion and be good for the soul. Can't it?

We started with an operatic song they had been working on the previous week. The group split into three part harmonies, and we repeated the same verse over and over again, "Will I lose my dignity? Will someone care for me? Will I wake tomorrow from this nightmare?" After repeating this monastic chant for fifteen minutes I was thoroughly depressed, wondering if someone from above was trying to send me a not very subtle message. Brighter tunes followed but I decided not to repeat the experience. My usual reclusive lifestyle was definitely a safer choice than risking the potential psychological trauma of village nightlife.

I carried on with my inner contemplation and waited for things to improve. Doors I tried to open seemed locked and I decided I would have to go it alone, both spiritually and musically. I sifted through a myriad of spiritual information on Youtube, without relating to any of it. Musically my goals were clearer. I would play by myself, sort out a personal busking system, make some backing tracks to play to and learn to make my own recordings. I got out the laptop, that Jimmi had loaded with recording software and took a look at it. I could get into the virtual desk he had loaded without a problem, but couldn't get any sound to come out, which was not very helpful. A message kept popping up about checking the plug ins, but I didn't know what it meant.

    I spent several days puzzling over it while researching microphones, amps, mixing desks and learning about phantom power, interfaces, dynamic and condenser mics, and various recording software options. The team at the Sax Company and GAK were endlessly helpful in suggesting the best options at affordable prices, but I still didn't know what software option to go for, or if I could use it on the soundless laptop. I sat with it, glaring at the annoying message while texting my sax friend Rich, from community radio, about the joy of being reunited with my repaired Selmer. He said he was about to go out to do see a friend, Neil, about some radio recording, who was a wiz on computers, I asked him whether he could mention the problem with my lap top.

    An hour later Neil called me and spent ages directing me to click on various options, to solve the problem, without any progress. Neil thought that Jimmi had been using an external sound card which had somehow corrupted the soft wear, and we decided the best option would be for me to send it to him to have a look at. Funnily enough it was this act of generosity, together with the help of several anonymous salesmen spending hours talking to me down the phone, which seemed to be a turning point in helping making me feel a bit better. While for the salesmen it was obviously about business, they had spent more time than they needed to trying to help me, even directing me on to different companies who they felt would meet my requirements better. As for Neil, there was nothing in it for him at all, he was just being kind, and I felt my trust in humanity being restored.

I sent the lap top to Neil and he quickly sorted it, and once I had phoned British Telecom to ask them to remove a confusing issue of orders from my home hub, it worked fine. I ordered a mic, interface, busking amp and various bits and pieces and when all the boxes of equipment arrived on the same day I panicked a little, doubting my ability to get anything operational. Once I'd calmed down and read the instructions I soon had the mic and amp plugged together and working. I had a condenser mic, which picks up all the soft breathy sounds of a sax and turning the dial to create a small delay made it sound amazing. It was soon echoing around the room like I was playing in some immense cavern and I couldn't stop playing it. Eventually I realised how late it was, and that my neighbours may not have quite the same appreciation for my sound system, and I reluctantly went to bed, the usual conveyor belt of work and domestic chores had to continue.

...

It was a normal Monday morning in the physiotherapy department. I was on my third patient when one of the office staff appeared with a serious face and told me I needed to phone the accident and emergency department of our local district hospital as soon as possible. Everything went into slow motion as I looked at her face, thought about my departure from the house a couple of hours earlier, leaving my son to catch a lift to school, thought about the foul weather that morning and realised what had happened. I left the patient in the cubicle and picked up the phone. Switch board put me straight through to A and E and then I was left listening to something that sounded like *Green Sleeves* while I waited for someone to pick up.

The sound track I was listening to gradually became more drawn out and distorted while my heart thumped louder and louder. By the time a couple of minutes passed the hope that my son had only been slightly injured, had spiralled downwards to him lying in a mangled heap, with a load of intravenous lines coming out of him, to possible death. At last the doctor came to phone. "Your son has been involved in a car accident, but he's okay, he's just a got a sore shoulder. I need your permission to release him from hospital."

The relief washed over me and as soon as I'd picked myself off the floor I drove over to collect him, somehow remembering to tell my patient to get dressed and come back next week. When I arrived there was nowhere to park and I abandoned the car on some double yellow lines and ran into A and E, to see my son coming towards me with a slightly embarrassed smile, his white school shirt covered in mud from where he'd crawled out the car. I hugged him.

"I was going to go to school mum, and do my exam, but they wouldn't release me without your permission and my shirt's a bit messy."

"I think we'll just go home." I said, and we left.

I was vaguely aware of my son's conversation, about what he'd learnt that morning about driving safely, as we drove home in the rain, when I suddenly realised there was something wrong with my eyes and I couldn't see properly. I'd been having further problems, in the last few months, waking with my left eye burning, stinging and watering profusely. Mr B had diagnosed me with nocturnal lagophthalmos, which sounded groovy, but simply meant I was sleeping with my eye open and the cornea had become dried out and scarred. He had given me some "gunk" to put in it at night and that had eased the problem, but as I blinked and opened and shut my eyes and tried to focus on the road, I realised it was my right eye that was the problem, and there was a pink veil coming over it, like when I'd had my previous retinal detachment.

I felt slight panic and disbelief, I couldn't see a safe place to stop, and then suddenly it cleared and went back to normal. I wondered if it was just stress and hoped it wouldn't come back, being blind in both eyes would be very limiting. We continue towards home and I looked out for the crash site.

"There it is," I said to my son, noticing a car lying on its roof in a field.

"No mum that's not it," we drove another hundred yards or so, "there it is" he pointed to a car lying on its side by the hedge. "Crikey there must have been another crash this morning," I said amazed at the madness of the days events.

We arrived home and I waited for my son to go into shock, but he seemed fine, while I went a bit wobbly, wondering how close it had been to him not being there. His mate turned up after school and I left them to talk while I went out into the front garden to do some weeding. I picked up the small brown recycling bin to put the weeds in and opened the lid.

"WTF!" I jumped in surprise. There was a small tabby cat curled up in the bottom on top of the vegetable peelings, on first glance it looked asleep, but from its lack of breathing I concluded it was dead. When I went back to work I discussed several theories, with Janey, on how it might have got there. It looked so peaceful it was almost as if it had lifted the lid, gone for a nap, and forgotten to wake up. We deliberated this against the possibility that someone had put it there, a road kill accident that had been furtively put in my bin. Both notions seemed a little odd, and we addressed the third theory, Janey's favourite, that I had been cursed; eventually deciding this was the most likely explanation. It looked a nice friendly cat, so maybe it was a lucky curse. I thought it was unfair to leave it to be recycled so tipped it out underneath some shady trees to decompose, and I wondered what would happen next.

I was unsurprised when the cat reappeared around the house. Its nature appeared to be that of a poltergeist intent on mischief, its first trick being to lock the toilet door from the inside. The door had done this once before about 18 months previously when Crazy had been living with me. Seb had been called and rescued us using male acumen. Since then the door had been fine, but now the latch dropped down on a regular basis, especially when the cat knew you were bursting to go.

Fortunately I had kept the cunning bit of cardboard Seb had used to slide in the crack in the door and flip the latch open. It still worked a treat, although sometimes needed to be done in a bit of a rush. I decided the cat must have a sense of humour, but the toilet trick was wearing a bit thin. I hoped the cat would be kinder to me when it came to the home recording project. I had now amassed the equipment I needed, but using it was proving challenging.

I managed to download the soft-wear required giving me a virtual recording desk, on my lap top, with lots of dials and drop down options which I didn't know how to use. Trying to follow self-help videos, on You tube was a slow and frustrating process, and I knew it would be much quicker to ask Jimmi to show me.

Over a month had passed since I'd spoken to him, but I'd thought about him a lot, and missed him. Jimmi was one of the few people I liked to spend time with and felt comfortable around; he had an innocent joy in the simple things of life, which made things seem like more fun when we were together. There was a dull ache where his friendship used to be and life felt flat and lonely without him.

Communication links had been briefly established when Jimmi had sent a text, apologising for losing his temper and enquiring how my son was after his accident. We exchanged a few polite messages, both hoping that things could be "cool" again between us. I thought about it for a week or so, I realised that Jimmi was not to blame for the upset that I had been feeling. I was responsible for my own thoughts and actions. Suddenly, on impulse, I sent him a text asking if he could help me out with my recording problems. It seemed like a fairly neutral way to approach him, rather than confronting the more emotional issues that had arisen following the weekend of "that" party.

Jimmi's response was quick and friendly, inviting me around to the flat. As I climbed the long flight of steps up to the back door I felt the tension rise in the pit of my stomach, remembering the last time I'd seen him. I wondered how things would be between us on this occasion.

I knocked and Jimmi appeared with a welcoming smile, looking better than I'd seen him for a long time. He'd been away and his health and state of mind had improved with the break. We sat and talked on his balcony for a couple of hours in the sunshine and said the things that needed to be said. Gradually some of the hurt melted away, and part of the huge weight that I had been carrying around inside of me, lifted. We went back to my house, and he sorted out my recording problems, laughing at the changes I'd made to the laptop, that he'd previously spent hours programming. We had some food together before he finally left. I sat down feeling rather drained by the emotions of the day, but glad that the hurdle of reconciliation had been crossed and we could move on.

The following week Jimmi started giving me some recording and mixing lessons. As we focused on the music the remaining awkwardness between us slipped away. Sitting with him on the beach one sunny afternoon, I thought that probably weren't many people around that I could watch limpets with, or could who could make me laugh making pretend limpet voices, or who I could stare at the clouds with, or ponder about the effect of aeroplane jet streams on climate change and radar waves.

We sauntered back to the flat and finished off some mixing some of the tracks I had been recording. Ally arrived and we all ate a Jimmi special of curry and chips, discussing the latest calamities life had thrown at us. Sitting on the balcony, laughing together in the evening sunshine, it felt like the world was returning back to normal again.

Only a few days later I felt ready to put Jimmi's recording lessons into action. After being taken with Adele's, *Rolling in the Deep*, I learnt it, ripped a backing track, recorded it, mixed it, and uploaded it on to SoundCloud. The mix wasn't right, the backing track I'd chosen had some distortion on it and I had struggled to get the sax to blend in with it and resorted to turning the levels up, which in turn had caused 'clipping'. Still, I was dead chuffed that I'd managed to remember all the processes and do it all by myself. I posted it up on Face Book and messaged Jimmi, who immediately pointed out the mix was all wrong. I felt deflated, but there again reminded myself that, that would be the first thing that Jimmi noticed.

The following day he came over and sorted out the mix on that and another track, *No Woman no Cry,* and managed to perfectly cook sausages and burgers on the barbeque that Seb and Jules had given me for Christmas. It was now June and the weather had finally become warm enough to eat outside. We idled the afternoon in the sunshine, the ache, reminding me of past events, had nearly disappeared, replaced by something nicer. Ally had already given me a number of "Be careful" warnings, about seeing him again, and as I watched Jimmi leave, the glow inside me faded and I decided it was definitely time to turn my attention back to the music.

Playing *No Woman no Cry* made me think it would be interesting to hire a tenor sax from the Windband and see what that was like to play. Some songs seemed more suited to it, than alto, but it would be heavier and bigger, with a larger mouth piece, which required a slacker embouchure. When I arrived back from Shrewsbury with my new toy, I put a shoulder harness on to take the extra weight. The tenor hung down somewhere below my crutch and felt miles too big for me. I blew into the mouth piece and soon managed to get down to the bottom note, but its size made everything hard work and after ten minutes I gave up and switched to the Alto.

Jimmi came round to have a look and after trying a bit of blowing down the tenor said, "Sod that for a laugh" and we had a cup of tea instead. He gave me a mixing refresh lesson, and I returned the favour by sorting out his back, which was bothering him, then we watched a documentary on Pink Floyd. It was all very domesticated and worryingly normal, except for the small tabby cat that stalked the floor.

The cat had become increasingly menacing. Having grown tired of the toilet trick it had taken to knocking things on the floor and breaking favourite ornaments. I tried to ignore it, and its rather antagonistic attitude towards me, hissing and bearing its claws, as I came through the door. I took to hissing back, before carrying on with what I was doing, which today was making Sunday roast. It wasn't something I did very often, but Jimmi was coming round to share the chicken stuffed with fresh lemon oregano from the garden and roasted vegetables. I was glad to see him, eating a roast dinner alone was not really worth the effort. It was much better shared with a friend, a friend that I now saw most days.

The chicken was ready and I was carving while Jimmi was making the gravy. The cat was mincing around the kitchen and I lost concentration of what I was doing, cutting my thumb with the sharp knife, blood pouring everywhere. I grabbed some kitchen roll and tried to stem the flow while mopping up the unattractive red pool that had spilt on the white plate waiting for the chicken. Eventually I managed to finish carving, without losing anymore digits, and we took the delicious offerings to eat in the sunshine.

After we finished I went back into the kitchen to make coffee in the percolator that Jimmi had given me. It was much more fun than the cafeteria to use and I watched it happily gurgling and spluttering on the hot plate. When it was ready I lifted the pot off the stove, keeping a wary eye on the cat sitting on the window sill. Distracted I spilt some of the boiling liquid from the spout, scalding the back of my hand.

The cat was proving to be a dangerous hazard in the kitchen and I retreated to the lounge, sitting with Jimmi, who was listening to the soul music he had downloaded from his memory stick. I'm not quite sure how it happened but one moment we were holding hands and the next we were kissing and hugging. I tried to resist, "I don't think this is a good idea," I finally managed to gasp. We talked for a while before gradually sliding back into the same clinch.

I was now definitely losing the fight with my conscience and the outcome seemed inevitable until, "Sh*t!", I leapt up in agony. Both my lower legs had gone into a vicious cramp and I hobbled round the room trying to release the spasm. The cat wished its tail, unsympathetically watching my efforts to relax my muscles. Eventually I was able to sit down again, but the break in the spell of intimacy was only temporary, it felt so good in Jimmi's arms. His phone rang and he turned it off. As we became locked again in another close hold I could see the cat's green eyes glaring at me over Jimmi's shoulder. The phone rang again. Saved by the bell, we both jumped up and came to our senses, agreeing it was time Jimmi should go.

"Well we just about stayed within the speed limit." Jimmi said brightly as he went out the door. I laughed, the cat hissed, and Jimmi was gone. I went and sat back on the settee, listening to the music. The Witch appeared.

"Good making out music," she said drily, "I see you've met Tiger." The cat purred and wrapped itself round her legs.

"Tiger?"

"Your guardian angel."

"I thought they were cute things with wings?"

"Tiger gets the job done better."

"Thanks," I said looking at the burn on my hand and the cut on my thumb, "guess it's my lucky day."

When I woke the next morning I was glad that things hadn't gone further with Jimmi and felt a little friendlier towards Tiger. Rather than risk his wrath again, I decided it would be better to stick to female company, and went to see Ally that evening, taking her a bottle of wine. Ally had decided she needed to get into training for going away on a short break, worried she wasn't fit enough to relive her former wild party days. By the time I left she had managed to drink the whole bottle of wine with consummate ease. I didn't think she would have a problem.

On the way back I stopped on the seafront, I still had Jimmi's memory stick and texted him, asking him if he wanted to come down for a late night walk. He waved down to me through his skylight and I could see he was on the phone. I waited and he eventually joined me looking upset.

"What's the matter?"

"Nothing."

His face was all crumpled and he started to cry.

"Was that Jane on the phone?" I asked, guessing.

"Yes," she's accusing me of stuff and doesn't even believe that I was with you yesterday evening."

Unfortunately it wasn't a surprise Jane didn't believe him. I hugged him, "Come on." We walked up and down the seafront in the quiet soft night, the only sound a small regular wave lapping on the shore and Jimmi's sobbing. By the time we got back to the flat Jimmi was calmer. We had some hot chocolate and I left, agreeing to come back and see him the next day.

I arrived the following afternoon to find Jimmi on his way back from a walk. When I caught up with him I decided it was time to do something daft to lift his mood and challenged him to a game of crazy golf. Having laughed our way around the course we went back for a pizza and then Sam turned up, in his cycling gear, and joined us for coffee and a smoke. Later as we watched Sam leave, weaving a slightly haphazard route down the road on his bike, Jimmi suggested we go for a walk down by the river. It seemed quite natural to walk along arm in arm, just close and warm together, without there being anything else. I took some pictures, trying to capture the moment of happiness on my phone.

On the way back to the flat Jimmi had noted a discarded long wooden box and bits of timber which we hauled up to the balcony. The box would be perfect as a planter and the timber could be used as a frame to make a mini poly tunnel. Jimmi craved the warmth of a sauna and got as far as buying a length of plastic sheeting, which he was wrapping around himself like a crisp packet. Making a frame to tack the plastic on and lean against the wall would make a far better job and be much more practical to use.

"Reckon the Gods are smiling on you," I said as we went inside. We sat in companionable silence drinking tea before reading our runes, picking one each out of the carved wooden box Jimmi kept them in. They were all about becoming complete and growing through our experiences. There had been a lot of experiences for both of us recently and I wondered whether we had moved on. I drove back home feeling peaceful and happy, maybe it was like Jimmi said "The hard road takes you to the best places". I unlocked my door, still smiling and drifted through into the kitchen, remaining calm even when Tiger smashed a bottle of beer on the floor in greeting. That cat didn't like me at all.

…

Jimmi came with me to Shrewsbury to swap the Tenor sax for a soprano, the tenor just too heavy and cumbersome. We laughed our way round Shrewsbury, took pictures, had coffee, I bought Jimmi some tomato plants and then we jumped back on the train home. It was a long hot intimate ride and on our return Tiger was up to his old tricks, making Jimmi lose the keys to my front door and temporarily paralysing him with a stitch in his side. Eventually we got in and I decided to ignore Tigers antics, after all, what did a cat guardian angel know about passion?

Later on as we sat eating and talking in the evening sun, Jimmi turned to me looking awkward, "Jane's invited me for dinner this weekend, I don't know what's going to happen, but…" I got his drift, from the way he emphasised "dinner", it sounded like he was hoping for deserts.

"Why didn't you tell me before we…?" I said in a low voice.

"Well I didn't know that…," I kept breathing while he staggered on to a rather feeble conclusion. We both fell silent into our thoughts.

I knew Jane had always been the special one and if there was a chance to make things work I knew he would take it. However, during my exchanges with Jane on Facebook, after "that party", she had said that she never wanted to be involved with him again. I hadn't seen it coming, but I guess she had changed her mind. I tried to balance this rational against the rising tide of feelings I had for Jimmi and what had just happened between us.

I was in shock but forced myself to carry on normally. I suggested we returned to his for some late evening poly tunnel building with the wood we'd found a few days previously. I could feel the hurt building inside of me and tried to hold it down hearing Ally's words in my head, "Whatever happens Jess don't give your heart to him." I didn't think I had, but as events of the last few weeks flickered through my mind I realised Ally's words were prophetic.

After we finished our woodwork we went in for coffee and read our runes, Jimmi's was good, about new beginnings, mine was less positive. Jimmi tried to change it by giving me more than one go, but it didn't matter it came up with the same reading - that I was in a repeating cycle but shouldn't get too hung up about it. Yeah, whatever. I left feeling hung up.

Early morning saw me back on the train again, this time heading off to work, having not slept at all. I found myself changing at Cyffordd Gythreuliaid, which feels like the platform at the end of the world. It is spookily hemmed in by marshland, from which there is no escape, except the metal tracks, which undoubtedly take you to the point where you fall off the earth into dark eternity. There was one other passenger on the platform, dressed in camouflage gear. He got a powerful telescope out of his rucksack and placed it on a tripod. He was probably keeping looking out for Nazgul from Mordor. Before they appeared Arriva trains boldly arrived at our outpost and I climbed slowly aboard one of the carriages. Despite being rescued from the swamp I was weighed down with the thought of the long tortuous weekend ahead of me, as I waited for the outcome of Jimmi's meeting with Jane.

Chapter 12. Shades of Grey

In tragedy, it's hard to find a good resolution; it's not black and white: it's a big fog of grey. (Paul Dano)

It was Saturday night, of the said tortuous weekend, and I was at Crazy's for a barbeque, huddled in a corner of the party shed while I told her the convoluted tale of my relationship with Jimmi. I seem to have been talking for ages. "So that's my story, and if I look stressed that's the reason why. I don't even know why it happened. It doesn't make any sense to me why I should fall for like a man like Jimmi, but we've shared all kinds of things, and he's made me happy when we're together. Now he's at Jane's tonight, probably getting back together with her, and I'm here at yours."

"Well you changed instruments, lost your connection with Jay, found one with Jimmi, the sax is much more his thing, and you've been hanging out together, making music, having fun." Crazy made it all sound inevitable, perhaps it was. I hadn't even thought about the significance of the change of instruments, which coincided with meeting the Witch and then bumping into Jimmi at the supermarket the day after I hired my first sax. The Witch, Jimmi, me and the sax were all connected, but why?

"Well, thanks for listening Crazy. I'd better go now, sorry I couldn't tell you before, it all just built up and then kept going. See you soon." I had a worrying feeling that I was becoming more crazy than Crazy, but since I'd only had a few hours' sleep in the last forty eight hours that was likely. I got back and fell into bed wondering what Jimmi was doing.

There was no word from Jimmi the following morning and I tried to keep my mind occupied with the soprano, which was proving much more comfortable and delightful to play than the tenor. It was a straight soprano, rather than curved, and I felt a bit like a snake charmer when I played it. It was less forgiving than the alto, any adjustments magnified by its smaller size, making tuning more of an issue. Being a B flat transposing instrument also meant the same fingerings were a different concert note to those played on E flat alto sax, and the embouchure was much tighter. Playing by ear I found adjusted to the fingering differences quite natural. I already knew I would be buying by own one at the end of the hire period.

In the afternoon I noticed a text pop up from Jimmi, enthusiastically inviting round for tea. I thought I knew what that meant, so I went round, steeling myself for what he was going to say. I sat in the corner of the kitchen while Jimmi bashed pans around and fried sausages and onions. Cooking was one of the ways he expressed himself and tried to show you he cared.

"…and that's what happened," he eventually concluded waving a spatula around. "It's not the same as before, and don't know how things are going to work out, but I'm trying to be honest with you and make things right this time."

"I understand," I said trying to be brave, and I did, but I wasn't very good at being brave and was fighting like mad to hold the tears back and hold my guts down by wrapping my arms around my body.

Jimmi saw my despair and hugged me while I sobbed quietly on his shoulder for a short while, before I sat back down in the kitchen chair and hung on it to tightly. I was grateful that Jimmi had been honest, this way we could still be friends and carry on seeing each other, but the anguish ran right through me. I knew that Jimmi would never be some kind of conventional partner, but our adventures together had awakened all sorts of emotions in me that could go no further.

He put a plate of food in front of me and I forced myself to eat a sausage, to show him I appreciated his efforts, somehow managing to swallow each thick lump of meat without choking. The conversation drifted backwards and forwards between discussing our feelings and less emotive topics, finally settling on the difficulties of transposing instruments and concert pitch. This felt a safe area to occupy our thoughts for a while, before I decided it was time to leave and bury my feelings for Jimmi in a safe box at the bottom of the garden. I walked to the door and Jimmi looked at me squarely.

"I love you."

"I love you too," I said and walked out the door and climbed slowly down the long flight of steps.

When I got back home I found I lacked the ability to do anything other than sit in the van. My last bit of energy had been used to walk away from Jimmi. I was incapable of opening the door and doing the next thing. I couldn't even think what the next thing might be, it felt too overwhelming. The trouble with Jimmi was that he made me feel. He made me feel all sorts of things, happy/sad, love/rejection, hope/despair, passionate/numb, emotions that I'd forgotten as I tried to extricate myself from my marriage and complicated relationship with Jay. Maybe that's what it was all about: feeling, experiencing, learning and becoming a more complete spirit. I turned to see the Witch was sitting beside me in the passenger seat stroking Tiger, who was purring on her lap.

"You really are a slow learner," she said.

...

A couple of days later I woke up feeling peaceful and happy, it was a beautiful day and I pottered around the garden and had a brief look on Facebook while I ate breakfast. There were some posts up on from Jay, and considering he was still in America and hadn't been on Facebook for weeks, I didn't think the timing was a coincidence. They were Buddhist teachings, all about accepting things as they were, rather than getting stressed because things weren't as you wanted them to be.

I did some music and went for a run, and then I went to see Jimmi and admire his finished efforts on his planter and poly tunnel. To my surprise I felt fine, we had a cup of tea, by the green oasis, and then went for a paddle on the beach, finally ending up sitting on the rocks, looking out to sea and talking. Well actually Jimmi did most of the talking, I just sat there enjoying the sparkling blue water and sky, the warmth of the sunshine on my skin, smelling the seaweed.

I felt as happy as I had felt distraught a few days previously, I felt good about me, good about the day, and good about Jimmi. I'd know him years and spent far more time with him this year than any other person. He was just part of my life and the space around me. Perhaps it was like he once sang, "we're just two lost souls swimming in a fish bowl, year after year", from Pink Floyd's, *Wish You Here*, and our friendship provided the companionship we both seemed to need. We wandered back to the flat and Jimmi cooked pizza, while I picked some salad, and we ate outside. Suddenly I felt really hungry and, for the first time ever, ate more than Jimmi. We were sitting having coffee, with Jimmi taking pictures of seagulls, when I realised he had turned and was pointing his camera at me.

"Look, that's how I see you," he said, picking out one of the shots and showing me in the view finder. I looked at myself, smiling back at me, a reflection of the happiness I felt at that moment.

A couple of days later Jimmi invited me over for tuna parmesan, a dish he hadn't cooked for me before. It was really delicious. Unerringly, as soon as coffee and desert appeared, so did Sam and his bike, this time with a flat tyre. After he had consumed his share of the offerings I took him, and his bike, back to Shady Grove, and then returned to discuss the music project I wanted to do with Jimmi. I'd been playing Petite Fleur for the past few days, on the Soprano, and inspired by my progress my thoughts had returned again to making a CD, an EP this time. I had five tracks in mind and I wanted to pass them by Jimmi and see what he thought.

Jimmi was enthusiastic and chipped in with ideas and we came up with a deal and he copied the files I'd been working onto his computer. As we were both now working in Cubase the transfer of material would be straight forward, and with my own mini studio it would all be a lot more easier than the first CD I had made, when I didn't really understand the processes involved.

I play him Petite Fleur, which I'd been having some problems with, trying to follow a version played by a clarinet. "You've got a lazy ear. It's in a harmonic minor scale, with that Arabic feel about it, due to the half steps. You take any whole steps and it ends up sounding English. I'm not going to let you get away with anything. I'll be like that teacher from Whiplash," he grinned, referring to the film we'd been to see a few months earlier. It featured a slightly mad drum teacher, determined to get the best out of his students by any means. Jimmi wasn't as obsessive, but his observations about music were just as astute.

It was nearly time to go and I put my hand in the rune box and pulled out one, Gebo, which signifies the gift of freedom from which flows other gifts. "Drawing this rune is an indication that partnership, in some form, is at hand. You are put on notice not to collapse yourself into that union. For true partnership is achieved by separate and whole beings who retain their separateness even as they unite. Remember to let the winds of heaven dance between you." I read out aloud. "Sounds like us, hopefully it's a good omen for the music," I smiled and left while the winds were still dancing.

Jimmi and I continued to hang out with each other, and usually everything between us was cool. I had stopped worrying about what our relationship was or wasn't. I just accepted it, enjoying our time together. Late one afternoon, after a trip out, we arrived back at the local supermarket to choose something for tea, when a text popped up from Jay, "I'm back". Somehow it seemed appropriate that his announcement arrived when I was out shopping with Jimmi. As I picked up a packet of cod I had a picture of Jay flash through my mind, arriving back at the airport wrapped in a robe, with a shaved head, (he had told me he had become a Buddhist). I wondered what the reality would be.

A couple of days later Jay called by for a cup of tea after I'd finished work. He was looking more American, than Buddha dressed in a smart jacket, jeans, and hat. I couldn't resist saying "Howdy" and we hugged and shared news. He'd had lots of adventures, including a hold up with a sheriff, a visit to a judge and an attorney, got off on all charges, and was finally home. Glad he'd been, but glad to be back in the softly falling Welsh rain and back in his own space.

Ironically although Jay had gone off in different directions, spiritually we seemed to have arrived in a similar place. The turmoil of the year had made me more open to wanting to learn from the experiences I was having and recently I had been on a two day psychology course at work about Mindfulness. This was very much in line with the Buddhist values that Jay felt affinity with.

We went out in the car park he proudly showed me the mandolin he'd brought back from the States, just like the one that Bill Monroe used to play. "Give us a tune, then," I encouraged him. He started to play and the tinkling notes immediately made me grab my violin from the back of the van and we played squashed between the parked vehicles. I hadn't played my violin for weeks, in fact I'd barely played it all year, I struggled to remember the tunes, but gradually they came back and the fingers started to remember, and it felt good to play together again, and good to play the violin. "See you around," I said and we parted.

...

Crazy thought it was time I moved on from the recent saga of my love life, and meet some other men, however she seemed short on solutions of how this was going to happen. I was having tea with her and Seb and they were both wracking theirs brains trying to think of some possibilities. "There is a man, who drives a lorry around who's really nice," Crazy frowned, trying to recall him.

"Is he single?"

"I think so."

"Do you know anything about him?"

"No, but he's really nice."

"How am I going to meet him?"

"Throw yourself under the lorry," was Seb's helpful contribution.

Crazy and I decided this might be potentially hazardous and that we needed to come up with some other possibilities which could end more happily than me being hospitalised.

"What about a dating website?" said Crazy looking inspired, "I know quite a few people who have met partners on the internet."

"Are you mad?" I said horrified at the thought.

That night as I lay in bed scrolling through my Facebook timeline, thinking how useless Crazy and Seb were as matchmakers, an advertisement for a dating website popped up, making me reconsider the idea. Well, why not, everything happened on the internet nowadays and the majority of the population were online, so I starting filling in my details, but after only completing less than half the form lost the will to live and courage to go any further.

An email popped up telling me I'd only completed 40% and needed to register. I didn't bother. Next moment another email had popped up thanking me for joining and suggesting a list of potential matches. Curious I scrolled down and saw a man who lived not too far away with an attractive picture and profile. I fiddled around with various options trying to find out more about him, and pressed an icon wondering what it did. Next moment I was told I had "winked" at him, I was alarm and embarrassed, unclear what I had done, I turned off the computer feeling very uncomfortable. The next day I had an email from the man I had winked at, but could only read the first four words because I hadn't paid a subscription to the site. My interest now piqued I reluctantly decided to join up for a month to learn what the rest of the email said.

The man introduced himself and we started a correspondence, which was all very well, but now because I had now signed up to the site it meant other men were viewing my profile, and winking at me. I found out this curious activity was a precursor that showed someone you were interested in them. I'm sure most of them were genuine but some were alarming, like the profile pictures posted by one man who was casually wrapped in his dressing gown on a four poster bed, and in another standing outside the front of an Ann Summers shop. He joined the list of definite no's (in a sub class of winkers I had re-labelled with a different vowel), along with the young, supposedly funny, man who'd quickly offered to give me a massage, the attractive black man who had described himself as white Caucasian, (in denial?) and the smooth talking Swiss man who, after smooching me with a few compliments, then creepily asked me if I trusted him. Our embryonic 'relationship' was four sentences long so the answer was, obviously not.

Cursing Crazy I hoped the month would be over quickly before my email box exploded with my 'Six of the day', or 'Twelve best matches', or I had a nervous break-down from the winker's and w#nkers. Unfortunately the trouble with the normal ones I chatted to was just that, they were too normal, it looked like dating web sites were not the way forward for me. It was time to get away and I headed to Llandudno Jazz festival for the weekend.

Of course Crazy had follow up advice for this event too, "Be brave and talk to people," she stated calmly. Obviously she was nuts, I'd gone to listen to music not to talk to anyone. When I arrived I discovered the average age of the audience was over seventy, and potential dates were limited, so I felt reasonably safe from any distractions. What I most wanted to do was to find some people to play with, hoping it might be like a Bluegrass festival where loads of people took their instruments and jammed. After I had driven several times around a windswept field in Llandudno I realised I was under a misconception. There was no one else camping with an instrument except me. I parked in the middle so I wouldn't disturb anyone else and played alone.

I went to check out the music enclosure, which was divided into two parts, the main performance tent and the jamming tent. The jamming tent sounded promising so I took my sax and went and looked inside. The compare was a guy called Ed, and there was a house band playing, with a singer. When they stopped for a break I had a chat with Ed.

"So this is your baby?" Ed asked, pointing to my sax bag.

"Yes."

"And you want to jam?"

"Yes"

"How long you been playing for?"

"About eight months."

"Ed went a bit pale under his black skin, "This is really meant as a jam tent for the professional players in between their sets on stage."

"Oh," I think Ed saw the disappointment in my face.

"Tell you what, have a listen to us and see what you think."

Ed got up and played with the band, he played alto sax and they did a few jazz standards. The band was very professional and could play any tune, in any key, without any rehearsal.

"So what do you think, you still want to play?" said Ed coming over to me again. He looked hopeful that he'd done enough to put me off, but I was desperate to play and felt confident that the house band was so adaptable there would be few problems.

"Yes, I do," I said determinedly and got up on stage with him. I might not have all the Jazz moves that years of experience gave you, but I could play with guts and sensitivity, which surely counted for a lot.

"*Summertime*, A minor concert," I said, on the basis I had played it many times and actually knew what key it was usually played in. Drawing to mind Jimmi's advice, "Keep it simple and play the basics well", I launched into it. I could hear Ed echoing and embellishing my lines, it sounded really good. I didn't want the pleasure of it to end, but it did and the audience clapped in appreciation. I would have loved to carry on, but Ed had singer coming on and I sat back down. A while later Ed invited me back to play *Mercy, Mercy, Mercy* with him and the singer. Oh good, I thought, as I'd played it before, in the standard key, however the singer usually chooses the key, which was something completely different. Before I had time to think about it she had started. I didn't know what the key was, and couldn't hear my self clearly enough to adapt. I felt uncomfortable, fortunately the singer did most of the song and I was glad when it was over.

Ed invited me back the following day to play a tune of my choice. I'd already bought an expensive ticket for the main tent, so wasn't going to hang out in the jam tent waiting for the off chance to play. Gratifyingly several people had come up to congratulate me on my performance of Summertime. They were even more impressed when they found out how little time I'd been playing. Unfortunately, though, jamming was over for the weekend. I went to listen how the pro's did it, hoping I'd get more chances in the future. The Brecon Jazz festival was only a few weeks away, so I thought I'd go and check that out.

I had booked to stay at the Brecon rugby club, which was very quiet and tranquil when I rolled up on Thursday afternoon. By Friday it was packed, mostly with people who were there for the fringe and didn't seem particularly into Jazz, judging by the ongoing rave that took place over the next 48 hours. Grateful I had been allocated a spot in the top left hand corner of the field I turned the van around to face the hills and tried to ignore the thump of the House music going on behind me.

I was practising my sax, in the van, when a lady with peroxide blond hair and a Valleys accent popped her head around the door. I stopped playing.

"Oh I love a sax," she smiled, "I said it was someone playing live and not a CD, but it did sound like a record. Can you play some more? It's bootiful."

I was finding it a bit disconcerting having a head poking through my van door. "Tell you what", I said "I'll come over to you in a bit, and play for you. It will be good practise for me." A short while later I wandered over to the group she was with. They were sitting in deck chairs enjoying the sunshine and drinking. I did a few tunes to my backing tracks, which they all seemed to enjoy judging by their accolades. Buoyed by their compliments I decided to do the open mic night that evening.

I arrived at the venue feeling confident, but was told playing to backing tracks wasn't the done thing. "You can play with me," smiled Bob. Since I'd only just met Bob as I'd walked through the door and had no idea what he was going to play, I wasn't entirely thrilled, but got up on stage with him.

Bob was playing acoustic guitar, plugged in, and singing something Bluesy. I managed to pick it up straight away and backed him up successfully, much to the surprise of both of us.

"Great I'll do another in that key," said Bob enthusiastically, and he did. "And another," he said appearing to enjoy himself, and he did. While I was glad I had managed to play three songs off the cuff, which I'd never heard before, it wasn't exactly what I had in mind. The evening passed without a chance for me to just get up and play a tune that I wanted to do.

Frustrated by the open mic, I decided the following day to busk. It would be the first time I'd busked by myself with the sax, and amp, and I was slightly intimidated by beginning my busking career at a prestigious event like the Brecon Jazz Festival. Late that morning I walked into town, cursing that I'd forgotten to bring a trolley with me and was struggling with a sax on my back and an amp under one arm. Feeling shy I went down a side street, which turned out to have the added bonus of being shady and having nice acoustics for the sax. Feeling nervous I started, soon feeling more relaxed, finding the sun glasses I was wearing particularly helpful in making me feel less self-conscious. I could see people stopping to listen, some money being thrown into my sax case and some stopping to talk. After a while, though, I realised as a thorough fare, it wasn't a great busking spot. I was going to have to be brave and go into the main market square.

The market was throbbing with activity, stalls crammed together; people in fancy dress, people on stilts, people selling food and drink, other buskers. There were demands on people's purses on every corner. I managed to find a good spot and set myself up. Lots of people were stopping to listen, take photographs and throw some change my way. The money wasn't important, in terms of its financial value, it was important as a sign of appreciation and it gave me a big confidence boost.

After about three quarters of an hour I was really getting into it, there were probably more people there for the Fringe, than the Jazz, and I was playing a variety of tunes to please everyone, but could hear a strange hissing sound. I wondered if I was standing on top of a gas leak, but then realised it was air was spilling out the corners of my mouth, as my muscles tired with the continuous playing.

In total I had probably blown for about two hours by then, with no one else to share the load, and it was time to quit while I was ahead. I'd made more than enough to pay for the three master classes I took that weekend. The rest of the time passed in a blur of sunshine and music; the exotic gypsy's of Taraf De Haidouks, the very droll tenor sax player Scott Hamilton, and the spontaneity and excellence of the late night jam.

As I slowly drove the van back over the hills I basked in the warm glow of the music and the compliments I had received for my own small musical contribution to the festival. I was glad I'd gone alone and been a one man band, standing or falling by my own efforts. It seemed the way forward for me in the future. I also found that now I had my own recording gear, and could put my own tracks up on SoundCloud, the urge to make a CD had diminished. The recordings weren't as good as the ones I'd done with Jimmi, but I could listen to myself anytime I wanted and monitor my progress. Musically I was now quite self-contained.

I still enjoyed spending time with Jimmi and a couple of weeks later we were sitting out on the rocks at the edge on the sea, it was one of those rare sunny afternoons that summer, warm and perfect. Jimmi sighed and stretched happily,

"This feels so blissful, it's like we're in another dimension, we must have known each other in a past life. Did you ever do any of Steve's regression therapies?"

"A couple," I said cautiously.

"What did you see?"

I briefly outlined my first experience.

"What about the second time?" he asked curiously.

I hesitated, unsure what to say to him.

"It's okay you don't have to say," he said sensing my discomfort. Jimmi had a sixth sense and I wondered again about the connection between him, myself and the Witch, and what Jimmi would think about it.

The afternoon continued to float by blissfully for both of us, except for the growing sense of unease in the back of my mind that I was enjoying Jimmi's company too much and his kisses were too sweet to resist. I thought back over the things we'd shared over the summer, and my attempts to distance myself from him, which had never lasted long for various reasons.

"You know every time I try to stop seeing you we end up in this situation again. The last two times it was due to you wanting to borrow the lap top, the time before that it was bumping into each other at the garage, when we were both going away, and the chances of us both being there for those same few minutes was very small."

"I know, it's mad isn't it," Jimmi agreed, "it's like we're two magnets attracted together by an irresistible force. "

I didn't know what the forces were, but they seemed stronger than I was. There was a big anniversary party coming up that weekend at Shady Grove and I was feeling increasingly anxious about it, and the thought of seeing Jimmi there with Jane. I had told Ally I wasn't going, but she gave me the third degree and I felt like a coward and agreed to go. I wasn't looking forward to it.

...

I left the party at 2am and went back home to sit in the dark and silence for a while. When my head cleared I picked up my lap top and began to write. The Witch sat next to me stroking a purring Tiger.

"So what about all the stuff you've left out?" she enquired, as I cut a big chunk out of the page in front of me.

I shifted uneasily and tried to change the subject, "I haven't seen Tiger for a while. Why's that?"

"Tiger only does black and white," she said enigmatically. I continued writing, keeping my eyes glued to the screen, wishing she wasn't so inscrutable and my life wasn't so difficult. I needed a break from the fog that surrounded me.

Chapter 13. The Fifth Dimension

These can't be the only notes in the world, there's got to be other notes some place, in some dimension, between the cracks in the piano keys. (Marvin Gaye)

George and I were sitting with our legs dangling over the harbour wall in Lower Fishguard. It was a beautiful afternoon, and the boats lay slack on their moorings as the sun beat down on the quiet water. I was eating curry straight out of the pan; the van was parked right behind me, surrounded by the boats on the hard. It was Thursday of the approaching bank holiday weekend, and having spotted there was a Jazz festival in town; it seemed a good idea to check it out.

"Very quaint, the boats and the sunshine remind me of Greece," said George admiring the view.

"It is pretty, probably a bit more Cornish than Greek, but home is where the heart is," I said innocently.

"Very droll," said George acidly.

"Sorry, anyway, you have always been very fond of Greece since your first grand tour of the Eastern Mediterranean."

"Indeed, coitum plenum et optabilem," he said dreamily.

I glared at him, "I wasn't referring to 'Greek love'."

"Certainly not!" George shook himself, "I meant I loved the marvellous landscapes, architecture, history and ancient treasures, treasures robbed by that despoiler Elgin."

"Yes, well, he'd completely lost his marbles," I said admiring my own wit.

George looked at me slyly. He had appeared to have recovered his composure from my indignant comment on his sexual preferences and began to idly recite some of his poetry from Don Juan.

And Julia sate with Juan, half embraced
And half retiring from the glowing arm,
Which trembled like the bosom where't was placed;
Yet still she must have thought there was no harm,
Or else't were easy to withdraw her waist;
But then the situation had its charm,
And then – God knows what next- I can't go on;
I'm almost sorry that I e're begun.

Oh Plato! Plato! You have paved the way,
With your confounded fantasies, to more
Immoral conduct by the fancied sway
Your system feigns o'er the controulless core
Of human hearts, than all the long array
Of poets and romancers:- You're a bore,
A charlatan, a coxcomb- and have been,
At best, no better than a go between

He finished, having managed to press all of my buttons with his prose. "So," I said irritably, "are you saying Plato was talking nonsense?"

"Haven't your actions proved my point completely?" he mocked. I didn't bother to reply. George had won our exchange of wit handsomely and I vowed not be so stupid as to provoke him again. "Let's go for a swim", I said changing the subject.

We walked down the quay side, past the old fisherman cottages, and the stone piece of art work, called the sun lover, who sat basking with his face towards the rays, before entering the water off the concrete steps next to the slip way. George was an excellent swimmer, once swimming right across the Dardanelles, but I found the water freezing and lost the feeling in my arms after a few strokes. It wasn't long before I was shivering under a towel, while George swam far out, using a powerful backstroke. I left him enjoying himself, and headed back to the van for a cup of tea.

As sat waiting for the kettle to boil I wondered why I hadn't visited this idyll before and where all the tourists were. There was no one else in the carpark, no signs demanding money or placing restrictions on the use of it, and I felt I had reached an undiscovered outpost which hard commercialism had yet to touch. George returned, "I think we'll stop here," I said to him, "its exclusive, cheap, you can't beat the view, there are facilities five minutes away and I can swim in the sea when I need a wash."

"Excellent," said George.

The next morning, after bacon and eggs, I decided to wander down to the internet cafe I had noted on the quayside the previous evening. It was a friendly place and as I chatted to the staff I learnt a bit more about the Jazz festival and an unlikely sounding activity called cardboard kayaking. The weekend sounded like it was going to be a lot more understated affair than the one in Brecon and later I drove into town to investigate.

I had hoped to busk, like in Brecon, but it soon became apparent Fishguard would not be a good place to do this as there was no obvious place to play. It was a linear town, the main road generating a lot of traffic noise and few pedestrians on the pavement. I went to get a programme and see what the weekend had to offer in terms of venues and bands. The upper town was rather run down, with abandoned shop fronts and improbable outlets, like the eccentrically named Edelweiss antiques. I was beginning to sympathise with the cars flashing past, before I discovered two gems, the very funky Ffwrn and a cool café/art gallery, Peppers.

Ffwrn was the nerve centre of Aber Jazz and as I walked in, through traditional chapel doors, I was unsuspecting of what lay behind them. The far end was dominated by a large bread oven and a bar, serving drinks and homemade food. Long wooden tables and chairs occupied the middle space, with comfy settees around the sides, ideal for viewing the stage at the near end. It was the best chapel I had ever been to. I asked one of the ticket staff if she knew any good spots to busk, but she had no idea, except suggesting I turn up later that afternoon and see if I could play in between the scheduled bands, and ask down at Peppers if I could play there.

I felt concerned about these possibilities; I preferred the independence of busking, which immediately meant I had to make myself do it as cowardice was not an option. I wandered down to Peppers and asked the owner, David, about it. He looked a bit bemused, but said I could play on Sunday afternoon, as they were having a barbeque. My venue booked I wandered back to the van to practice for the chance of playing at Ffwrn later that day. Unfortunately, my rehearsal failed to inspire me as I struggled with every tune I attempted. After a couple of hours I felt like bottling it, but I forced myself to front up at Ffwrn. It would surely be alright on the night.

As it turned out, I need not have worried and I wished I had listened to my inner demons telling me not to do it. There were not many people around, and after asking the owners whether I could play, I hopped up on stage, set up my mic, closed my eyes (having forgotten my sunglasses) and launched into a Blues number. When I opened my eyes, ten minutes later, Rhodri, one of the owners of Ffwrn, was standing there, looking apologetic, "That was really lovely, it really was, but the next band have arrived and need to set up." I looked in the direction that he pointed, and saw three guys standing awkwardly with a load of music gear. I quickly jumped off the stage feeling embarrassed.

Peppers turned out to be better experience; I played outside the entrance, had plenty of time and could run it as I wanted.

After about an hour I tired, I had played for my supper, and while my tuna cooked on the barbeque I went to the bar to get a drink. A couple of men sitting at a table nodded to me, "Nice playing," said the tall thin one, with his grey hair in a pony-tail.

"Thanks," I smiled adding it to the other kind remarks I'd received, and thought no more of it. Later I was chatting to the other man who had been at the table, as we waited for the Steve Jones quartet to start. "Do you know who the man at the bar is who complimented you?" he asked me.

"No, "I shrugged.

"Nick Turner, who played with Hawkwind, he's a pretty good sax player himself... Err you have heard of Hawkwind haven't you?" he checked.

"Yes, of course," I said, and had a flash back to the legendary psychedelic space age rock band thrashing on their guitars to their massive hit, *Silver Machine*. In a far out band Nick Turner was the farthest out of all, but before I got too distracted with the images in my mind, the Steve Jones quartet drew me back to the present, and their tribute to Miles Davis, Seven Steps.

Miles Davis is widely recognised as one of the most significant musicians of the twentieth century, his contribution to Bebop, Hard Bop, Cool, Modal and Fusion Jazz influencing many musicians outside of Jazz, while his album, *Kind of Blue*, remains one of the best-selling Jazz albums of all time. *Kind of Blue* was recorded in only seven hours. All of the tracks, except one, were first takes, on the basis that first thought is best thought. The haunting tunes showcase Miles' distinctive trumpet style; introspective, lyrical, and sexy. His intimate sound is achieved by his use of a mute, a technique that is said to have been so seductive it made ladies in the audience swoon and unconsciously open their legs a little wider.

    His early career was forged playing Bebop with Charlie Parker before he went on to develop a more stripped back style, becoming master of the attention grabbing "harmonic bomb", which he dropped to break an audiences trance and take them to a different place. I found myself in a peaceful place listening to the Seven Steps to Heaven homage, charmed by the little boy also rapturously enjoying the session. Granted his dad was playing, but he was obviously appreciating the whole piece. Speaking to his mother afterwards she said it was what he had been brought up with. He showed no interest in pop music at all, even requesting Thelonious Monk to be played in the car. "Mind you," she said apologetically, "his little sister does prefer Beyoncé." The two contrasting musical styles were a startling but amusing thought, as I imagined what their car journeys must be like.

    After the quartet had finished I returned to Ffwrn to listen to the headlining band, Red Stripe. They were stomping boogie woogie band, and brilliantly entertaining, at one stage jumping into the audience, with the baritone player standing on one of the tables taking a solo, while later Nick Turner joined the action, cutting a break on one tune. Red Stripe's engaging style made it impossible not to clap and dance to their groove and I returned late to the van my feet still tapping.

The following evening I went down to the quayside to play, just for fun, hopefully adding a little to the festive atmosphere of the final climatic experience of the Bank Holiday Monday, card board kayaking. For some reason Bank Holidays seem to bring out a certain streak of madness in the British public and a variety of craft had been prepared to take part in the occasion, my favourite being Fishguard Herrings, cleverly designed as an open tin of fish with the lid rolled back with a giant key. Some vessels sank fairly rapidly, the occupant bravely paddling on while sitting encased in a box of sinking cardboard, while others floated for an extraordinary length of time, making me wonder about the judges pre-competition vetting of the entrants and the amount of duct-tape used.

The competition ended with a demolition derby, and I noticed the Clubbing Lunatics purposefully paddling out to join the fray in a magnificent Viking longboat. Each of them wore a Viking helmet with large cow horns, and heaved on long wooden oar. Their efforts propelled the boat through the water at quite a speed, until Ugg caught a crab, causing their rhythm to stutter and the boat to stall. Ugg blamed Nugg, who blamed Fump, who turned around and hit Wump over the head with his paddle. A fierce brawl broke out, they all traded blows, and the boat's dragon head was cut off by a swinging chop from Nugg. Their battle hastened the demise of their vessel, which rapidly disintegrated under the assault. They sank with much shouting and splashing, before they began a long, dismal, and argumentative, swim back to shore.

Eventually there was only one craft left floating, and as the sun set on the quay side strewn with the soggy remains of the competitor's crafts, I decided it was time to leave. I had now been living in the car park for four nights, and a town pay and display during the day. Although I considered a tour of Welsh carparks, to see if they were all as accommodating, duty called and I headed home.

...

On my return Muttley had come down to stay with Jimmi, and I was looking forward to seeing him. It was a year and a half since he had last visited and in the meantime I had taken up the sax and was hopeful of some tips and a bit of a jam. Muttley was obliging and I had a few entertaining days with him and Jimmi, before he returned to Liverpool. As the three of us lay on our backs on the floor of Jimmi's flat, after a rather magical pizza, they felt like my brothers and best mates, all rolled into one. I wished Muttley could have stayed, not only for his company, but his great sound on the soprano. It had inspired me to pay more attention to the one I had hired and a couple of weeks later I returned to Shrewsbury to purchase my own. Muttley had left me his old flute to try, but I didn't think I would have time to practise that as well, and for the time being it lay on the shelf as a memento of his visit.

Once Muttley had gone I drifted back into seeing Jimmi again, sharing with him my new found pleasures in gardening and cooking, having meals together, doing some music, going for walks, eating ice-creams, picking blackberries, making pies. It was a golden autumn, the streaks of sunlight making the bubble which surrounded me sparkle and glitter. The light made it hard to see properly and my judgement became impaired. The glittering bubble floated on in the breeze unconcerned with such trivia.

Suddenly there was a reality check and the outside world intruded in the form of Ally's birthday party. I was relieved when Jimmi said he wasn't going, but later that evening he turned up with Jane, taking me by surprise. By 3 am the last few people were all dancing to Stevie Wonder, but I couldn't move from my seat due to the heavy weight in the pit of my stomach. The bubble had burst, and when finally I managed to stand, I made my way out into the dark night and started up my van.

After fifteen minutes of trying to manoeuvre around the parked cars I found I had wedged myself into a corner, not able to go forward or back, it felt symbolic of my relationship with Jimmi. To my distress, I had to go back into the house and ask him to extract the van for me. Ally came out and insisted I stay, even if she had to sacrifice herself by throwing her body under my wheels. I felt this was a bit dramatic, my mood had left me stone cold sober and I felt fine to drive, but I didn't want blood all over the tyres so I stayed, shivering in my sleeping bag, and leaving as soon as the sun came up.

I drove through the sepia countryside to Cadair Idris, parked up, and made a reviving cup of coffee. While the kettle boiled I picked up a text from Jimmi, sent the previous evening, warning me about the change in plan. I'd been out of signal and it had arrived too late, I'm not sure it would have made any difference to how I felt anyway. I got changed into some clothes more appropriate for mountain walking, and set off. It was only a week since I had last climbed Cadair, but this time my mood was different, and I had a strange disembodied feeling, watching my legs move underneath me but not feeling connected to them.

As I got higher, neither the cold blue autumn sky, or the perfect reflection in the lake, lifted my spirit. I paused half way up the stone chute to retch on my empty stomach. I wasn't sure whether it was the previous evenings interesting combination of wine, cider and vodka, or the lack of food, but I ignored its protest and continued on my way. Eventually I arrived back at the carpark, feeling little different to when I had left it a few hours previously, there are some things you can't walk away from.

…

The weather stayed fine and I went out sailing, pulling the main sheet in hard as I beat against the outgoing tide and wind, making slow progress. Eleanor appeared standing on the bow holding onto the mast. She turned to me and smiled, "This is getting a bit tedious, it's time to tack, change direction, and have some fun." She was right; I moved the tiller across and turned, letting the sail out onto broad reach. As my speed increased I shifted my weight back, the bow lifted, the friction decreased and the boat started planing.

I leant out to balance the power in the sail and the cold water splashed my face exhilarating me. In less than thirty seconds I had skimmed across the water to the far shore. Eleanor's hair streamed out behind her and she laughed with the thrill of the ride, "That's better; lighten up, the winds are changing, go with them, it's time to move on and finish this book.

"Is it going to have a happy ending?" I asked hopefully.

She laughed, "What do you think this is, a fairy tale?"

It was all very well for the Witch to say "move on", but so far events had conspired against me as I tried to continue my friendship with Jimmi whilst avoiding the pitfalls of emotional entanglement. I had tried my best, but sometimes my best wasn't good enough. I had to stop kidding myself that we could just be friends. I loved him, and the balance of friendship was too hard to strike.

I was in a similar repeating cycle with him to the one I had been in with Jay, except now our roles had been reversed. Despite the Witch's warning I had made the same mistakes all over again. I had to break the cycle before my integrity and happiness were completely wrecked by the emotional rollercoaster I was riding. The only way appeared to be to stop seeing him, probably for a long time, but up to now I hadn't been able to keep the resolutions I'd made.

I was reflecting on this while writing on the seafront one a hot, blue day at the beginning of November. The Witch was prancing around on the seawall, offering no help in solving my dilemma. Suddenly she turned and did a very witchy thing. Producing a wand, and with a flourish, pointed it towards me. There was a flash and my mobile went off. It was Jane. I had been thinking about her but hadn't expected to hear her voice asking about my relationship with Jimmi.

I had known Jane for years as Jimmi's main girlfriend. I liked her, but I had never really talked to her. Today was no different; I didn't even know where to begin explaining my relationship with Jimmi except that it was "complex". Long pauses hung in the air while I scrabbled around for words to stick together in a sentence. It was during one of these silences that I suddenly I realised an escape route from my repeating cycle with Jimmi was at hand. There was a high cost to pay, but I would have to pay the price. I forced myself to say the words out loud, "I am not going to see Jimmi anymore." Once I said it there was no going back.

I put the phone down and sprawled out across the back seat of the van, suffocating under a heavy blanket of emotions, the afternoon sun dazzling me through the open door. The CD player was playing Charlie Parker with Strings, and moved through the tracks of my year with Jimmi: *Just Friends, Out of nowhere, Easy to love, Summertime, Temptation, What is this thing called love? If I Should Lose You.*

It went through the 24 songs of the album twice, before I could stir myself, then I took my sax down to the rocks and played the Blues to the setting sun. I would never see Jimmi, or play music with him again; the finality was devastating. I went home and cried, and Crazy came round and hugged me, and I cried some more. She shared my pain, fixed my lights, made me a cup of tea, and once I was able to laugh about the next possible misfortune that might befall me, she left. I picked up my lap top and began to write.

So here I am, finishing this book. It's one o'clock in the morning and all the gang are here: Eleanor, Bird, Ugg, Nugg, Wump, Fump, listening attentively to George as he strides around the room, expansively waving his arms and spouting his poetry.

There's music in the sighing of a reed
There's music in the gushing of a rill
There's music in all things, if men had ears
Their earth is but an echo of the spheres

Bird nodded in agreement, *"I kept thinking there's bound to be something else… I could hear it sometimes, but I couldn't play it."*

I went outside into garden to consider his words. He was right, there was something else, and you couldn't always play it, or even understand it. But if you listened carefully you could hear it, and if you opened your soul, you could feel it.

I thought back to earlier in September, picking blackberries in the wood with Jimmi. We had pushed our way deeper into one of the bushes to try and get the bigger berries. The brambles cracked under my feet, and the juicy fruit was damp as I pulled it off the stalk. There was a timeless feel to woods, the decay of the dying leaves providing nourishment for the ground which the plants used to grow the fruit containing new life. I looked up and pointed out to Jimmi the blue skies in the break of the twisted tree branches above us, "Yes, we're in that other dimension again," he said.

We finished picking and sat on a wooden bench, continuing to enjoy the peaceful, earthy atmosphere of the encircling plants and trees, the soil, grass and tangled bushes. An old woman and a rather tatty looking grey and white dog walked by, we had met them both earlier on the path. She greeted us again and shook her full pot of blackberries at us, "Enough there for a pie," she beamed; it felt like we were all connected to the wood.

I experienced a sudden shaft of realisation, and turned to the Witch, who had now joined me in the garden, "That was you, wasn't it?"

"Yes, of course, I often hang out in the fourth dimension, in transit to the fifth," she smiled.

"The fifth dimension?"

"Cosmic consciousness when your mind lets go of the everyday distractions and becomes deeply connected to the source. It's a feeling of an effortless flow of life; everything is more real and brighter, it's an upgrade on the fourth dimension."

"The fourth dimension is time, according to Einstein's theory, isn't it?"

"Yes, but that's a measureable, linear view of time. Was there any concept of time in the woods?

I thought about it, "Well no, it was timeless, just the moment."

"And it's 'the moment' which takes you closer to the source."

It was those moments of awareness that I'd loved sharing with Jimmi. As well as bringing into focus the detail of the landscape around me and a greater spiritual awareness, he'd helped put me back in touch with my feelings, taught me about the pleasure of growing herbs and tomatoes, the practicalities of how to make good coffee, banana pancakes and dahl, the benefits of Himalayan salt, musically about playing on the edge and in the groove, and how to record and mix.

Looking back over the year and the time we'd shared together, it had been one hell of a ride. Over recent weeks I had reached a more reflective understanding of this, but the musical thread, brightly woven between us, had now been abruptly severed. I would have to travel on without him. I wondered whether I would share my future journey with anyone else and whether I'd reach the fifth dimension.

"So, are you off to Africa in the New Year?" asked Eleanor breaking into my thoughts.

"Yes, I'll be working on a Wales for Africa project, only for a couple of months, but who knows what I'll find out there. How about you, do you think you'll ever make it to Egypt?"

"Maybe," she shrugged, "arriving doesn't really matter; it's all about the experiences on the way and heading in the right direction." She rammed a black pointy witch's hat on her head, and clicked her fingers; a broomstick appeared hovering above the ground. She got on, fidgeting about trying to get comfortable. "Anyway, thought I'd see how far I'd get on this," she said, gripping the handle tightly. There was a compass strapped to the end and she purposefully set the dial, "I've always wanted to see the pyramids", she said excitedly, and took off. Moments later a silhouette of her sitting on her broomstick flew across the large silver moon hanging in night sky. She did a rather precarious loop-the loop, nearly falling off, before successfully recovering her balance and heading off south towards Egypt.

Postscript

A couple of weeks later a post card, with a picture of the Great Sphinx of Giza, came through my letter box. It was from the Witch.

Made it! Epic trip, my butt is totalled, can't even think about a camel ride.
Pyramids amazing, had lunch in one yesterday with some Mummies.
Taking a cruise down the Nile, will catch up with you in 2016 when you get to Africa.
All the best,
Eleanor xx

Made in the USA
Charleston, SC
24 November 2015